CHARACTER ENCYCLOPEDIA

WRITTEN BY SIMON HUGO AND CAVAN SCOTT

CONTENTS

ENTER
THE WORLD OF LEGO®
DC COMICS SUPER HEROES!

Brave LEGO® DC Comics Super Heroes take many forms –
from the superpowered to the purely courageous with high-
tech gear and gadgets. The villains they face are dangerously
varied – and their minifigure counterparts are equally so!

HOW TO USE THIS BOOK

This book is a comprehensive guide to ten years of LEGO DC Comics Super Heroes
minifigures, vehicles and explosive sets! Minifigures and vehicles are ordered
chronologically according to when they were released, from 2006–2016.

BRUCE WAYNE
TO THE MANOR BORN

VITAL STATS
....

LIKES: Bats
DISLIKES: Bats (Bruce is a complex guy!)
FRIENDS: Alfred
FOES: Anyone who might discover his secret identity
SKILLS: Brilliant businessman
GEAR: Secret hideout

SET NAMES: The Batcave: The Penguin and Mr Freeze's Invasion
SET NUMBERS: 7783
YEARS: 2006

DID YOU KNOW?
Wayne Enterprises includes Wayne Technologies, Wayne Medical, Wayne Foods, Wayne Weapons, Wayne Airlines, Wayne Energy, Wayne Entertainment and more!

Classic LEGO® hair, around since 1979!

Same smirk as Colonel Hardy (p.91)

Sharp suit also used in LEGO® Indiana Jones™ theme.

BECOMING BATMAN
A bridge in Bruce's Batcave leads to a gym and a chamber where Bruce can change into his Batsuit. But beware! It also has a trapdoor to a cage below.

Bruce is the billionaire boss of Wayne Enterprises. He raises money for charity through the Wayne Foundation, throws lavish parties and often features in Gotham City's gossip columns. (He's also secretly Batman – but don't tell anybody!)

BATMAN
THE MAN IN BLACK

DID YOU KNOW?
An exclusive San Diego Comic-Con giveaway in 2005 included this version of Batman along with the Joker (see p.24).

VITAL STATS
....

LIKES: Gotham City
DISLIKES: Crime
FRIENDS: Commissioner Gordon
FOES: The Joker
SKILLS: Scaring bad guys
GEAR: Bulletproof armour, Utility Belt

SET NAMES: The Batmobile: Two-Face's Escape, The Batcave: The Penguin and Mr Freeze's Invasion, Arkham Asylum
SET NUMBERS: 7781, 7783, 7785
YEARS: 2006

BAT PACK
Batman can't fly like Superman, but when the Riddler, Scarecrow and Poison Ivy break out of Arkham Asylum (set 7785), he tracks them down using this giant bat-shaped jetpack.

Pointy bat ears for a scary silhouette!

Armour moulded around muscles

Utility Belt can carry grapple gun and smoke bombs

Batman is the protector of Gotham City. When the Bat-Signal shines in the sky, he answers the call to action – sweeping in from the shadows or blasting onto the scene in his Batmobile.

BATMAN
THE CAPED CRUSADER

VITAL STATS
....

LIKES: Big pockets for tools
DISLIKES: Criminals running amok in Gotham City
FRIENDS: Robin
FOES: The Riddler, Bane, Scarecrow
SKILLS: Criminology
GEAR: Bat-cuffs

SET NAMES: The Batcopter: The Chase for Scarecrow, The Bat-Tank: The Riddler and Bane's Hideout
SET NUMBERS: 7786, 7787
YEARS: 2007

DID YOU KNOW?
There have been at least 30 different bat-symbols since Batman's comic-book debut in 1940.

Blue cowl looks good in the moonlight!

Simple bat-symbol

Chunky Utility Belt

2007

Lead-lined cowl

Arched bat-symbol

Five-pointed cape echoes bat-symbol

VITAL STATS
....

LIKES: Not being seen
DISLIKES: Smiling for photos
FRIENDS: Alfred
FOES: The Joker, Catwoman, Killer Croc
SKILLS: Nighttime camouflage
GEAR: Batwing launcher

SET NAMES: The Batman Dragster: Catwoman Pursuit, The Batboat: Hunt for Killer Croc, The Batwing: The Joker's Aerial Assault
SET NUMBERS: 7779, 7780, 7782
YEARS: 2006

2006

Listening device in right ear of cowl

Flexible kevlar armour

2008

Utility Belt includes Tumbler remote control

COMIC CHARACTER

At the San Diego Comic-Con in 2011 this exclusive Batman minifigure was released to mark the relaunch of the LEGO DC Comics Super Heroes range. His armour is darker and tougher.

DID YOU KNOW?

All Batman minifigures released before 2011 have the same face printing, with serious eyes, a stern mouth and a white sweatband.

The Caped Crusader dresses to impress, updating his outfits as crime fighting fashion dictates. Blue, black and grey are his go-to colours, with a belt to add a bit of bling. While the details may change, the iconic cape and cowl mean he's always unmistakably Batman!

BATMOBILE
BACK IN TOWN

VITAL STATS

OWNER: Batman
USED FOR: Catching crooks
GEAR: Mega-missile

SET NAME: The Batmobile: Two-Face's Escape
SET NUMBER: 7781
YEAR: 2006

Flexible fins shaped like bats' wings

Power flows to all four wheels via chunky pipes

Lever launches missile

Rubber-nosed missile

Headlights are stickers

BATMAN'S BUGGY

The Caped Crusader pursues another crook in Batman's Buggy: The Escape of Mr Freeze (set 7884). His Buggy is smaller than the Batmobile, but still stops traffic with its built-in gadgets.

This version of the Batmobile packs a real punch, with a huge missile loaded between the front wheels. When Batman uses this surprise weapon against Two-Face, it blasts the villain right off the roof of his getaway truck!

BATMAN DRAGSTER
FOR GOING ON A LONG DRIVE

Tail fin reduces drag

DID YOU KNOW?
The fastest racing dragsters can reach speeds over 300 miles per hour!

VITAL STATS

OWNER Batman
USED FOR: High-speed chases
GEAR: Missiles, laser cannon

SET NAME: The Batman Dragster: Catwoman Pursuit
SET NUMBER: 7779
YEAR: 2006

Rotating laser cannon

Missile launcher

Cooling vent

CANNON-FACING
A hidden front wheel steers the dragster left and right. The laser cannon turns with the wheel, so that it is always pointing to wherever the dragster is going.

Batman built this dragster for speed. Where wider vehicles are slowed by the wind, this dart-like design can slice through Gotham City's streets like a scythe. Its shape and speed also make it a hard target to hit in a battle.

ALFRED
BATMAN'S BUTLER

Bald head accompanies wise expression

Classic LEGO goblet for taking refreshment to Batman

Alfred's suit rivals those of the Penguin's!

SOME ICE, SIR?

Alfred rarely battles bad guys, but when the Batcave is attacked, he doesn't lose his cool. In fact, he seems positively chilled when Mr Freeze traps him in a block of ice!

Alfred Pennyworth is one of the few people trusted with Batman's biggest secret: his other identity as Bruce Wayne! He provides loyal service at Wayne Manor – and beneath it in the Batcave.

ROBIN
TRUSTED SIDEKICK

Flat hairpiece has also appeared in LEGO® Pharaoh's Quest and LEGO® City sets.

Both 2006 and 2008 Robin minifigures variants wear the same outfit with a bright yellow cape.

"R" on chest is a stylized throwing star

BIRD ON THE WATER

The Boy Wonder made a splash with a different hairstyle when he sped into battle on his jet ski in The Batcave: The Penguin and Mr Freeze's Invasion (set 7783) in 2006.

When Tim Drake realised that Batman needed help, he used his detective skills to work out the Caped Crusader's secret identity. Batman was so impressed with Tim's abilities that he trained him to become his sidekick – Robin.

THE BATCAVE

The first of three LEGO Batcaves, this design, from set 7783, features a Batcomputer displaying Batman's Rogues Gallery and a Mr Freeze intent on trapping Alfred the butler!

THOOM!

NAME: Harvey Dent
ALIAS: Two-Face
BASE: Unknown

THE PENGUIN? MORE LIKE THE CHICKEN! STOP RUNNING AWAY!

ROBIN'S SCUBA JET
THE BOY WONDER GOES UNDER

VITAL STATS

OWNED BY: Robin
USED FOR: Deep-water diving
GEAR: Breathable atmosphere, rocket launchers

SET NAMES: Robin's Scuba Jet: Attack of The Penguin
SET NUMBERS: 7885
YEARS: 2008

Colour scheme with "R" symbols matches Robin's costume.

BIRD STRIKE

Robin knows when he's close to the Penguin's Submarine. That's when the Penguin sends his robot helpers to attack. These robo-penguins work just as well under water as on land!

Blaster weapons designed to work underwater.

Large, clear canopy gives Robin a wide sea-view.

These green engines do not appear in any other LEGO set.

Robin can breathe easy as he dives deep in pursuit of the Penguin. His Scuba Jet has its own air supply so he can stay underwater for extended periods – although its twin turbine engines should bring any chase to a speedy end.

NIGHTWING
SOLO FLYER

VITAL STATS

LIKES: Acrobatics
DISLIKES: Being told what to do
FRIENDS: Batman
FOES: Poison Ivy
SKILLS: Martial arts
GEAR: Escrima sticks

SET NAMES: Arkham Asylum
SET NUMBERS: 7785
YEARS: 2006

Rubber hairpiece created for LEGO® EXO-FORCE™ theme in 2006.

Mask shaped like wings spread in flight

Blue and black costume also echoes the wingspan of a bird or a dragon.

NIGHT RIDER

Nightwing rides this streamlined bike to help Batman foil an escape from Arkham Asylum (set 7785). It has space for his two martial arts fighting sticks, also known as escrima, at the back.

Dick Grayson was the first Robin, fighting crime alongside Batman. As he grew older, he wanted to go his own way. He chose Nightwing as his new identity after Superman told him about a legendary Kryptonian character with the same name.

CATWOMAN
GOTHAM CITY'S NUMBER ONE CAT BURGLAR

VITAL STATS

LIKES: Diamonds
DISLIKES: Getting caught
FRIENDS: Batman
FOES: Batman
SKILLS: Quick getaways
GEAR: Whip

SET NAMES: Catwoman
Catcycle City Chase
SET NUMBERS: 6858
YEARS: 2012

DID YOU KNOW?

Catwoman appears in all three of the LEGO® Batman video games, along with her cat, Isis.

Mask doubles as a Catcycle helmet

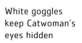

White goggles keep Catwoman's eyes hidden

Catwoman's 2012 costume comes complete with a chunkier zip and belt.

LITTLE BLACK CATSUIT

Catwoman's 2006 minifigure wears a stealthy black catsuit with a matching black mask and simpler torso detailing. Armed with her trusty whip, this cat burglar is ready to tangle with Batman in The Batman Dragster: Catwoman Pursuit (set 7779).

Glamorous Selina Kyle has a weakness for glittering diamonds. No gem is safe while Catwoman is on the prowl. A talented gymnast, Selina often has to make acrobatic escapes from Batman.

CATCYCLE
MEEEEEOWWWWW!

VITAL STATS
....

OWNER: Catwoman
USED FOR: Cat burglary
GEAR: Whip

SET NAME: Catwoman Catcycle City Chase
SET NUMBER: 6858
YEAR: 2012

Stolen diamond

In-built grip for a whip

Kickstand in raised position

EYES ON THE ROAD
The Catcycle in The Batman Dragster: Catwoman Pursuit (set 7779) has cat's eyes and ears at the front and an exhaust flame trailing like a cat's tail.

Speeding like a cheetah, Selina Kyle's catlike bike can whisk her from crime scene to crime scene with barely a pause. Her two wheels purr along nicely – whether she's driving to commit the crimes or solve them.

KILLER CROC
COLD-BLOODED CROOK

VITAL STATS

LIKES: Wrestling alligators
DISLIKES: People making fun of his appearance
FRIENDS: The Penguin
FOES: Batman and Robin
SKILLS: Fast healing
GEAR: Gun

SET NAMES: The Batboat: Hunt for Killer Croc
SET NUMBERS: 7780
YEARS: 2006

Exclusive scaly face printing

Narrowed red eyes

Scales continue on unique torso printing.

SCALE MODEL

Killer Croc does his best to outpace the Batboat in this small speedboat. Part of the character's only LEGO set appearance to date, it features exclusive crocodile-face printing and swamp-green missiles.

With a grin to rival the Joker's, this reptilian rascal could snap at any moment! He may not have much in the way of brains, but his tough, scaly skin and super-strength make him the mean, green king of Gotham City's swamps.

THE BATBOAT
BAT ON THE WATER

VITAL STATS
••••••••••••••••••••••••
OWNED BY: Batman
USED FOR: Swamp chases
GEAR: Built-in jet ski

SET NAMES: The Batboat:
Hunt for Killer Croc
SET NUMBERS: 7780
YEARS: 2006

Bat-shaped wings leave no doubt who owns this craft!

Twin propellers are linked and turn together.

Space to store jet ski behind cockpit

CRAFTY GETAWAY

A one-person jet ski fits into the back of the Batboat. Small enough to speed along narrow rivers or even sewers, it's the perfect craft to pursue Killer Croc's speedboat.

This heavily armed hovercraft is ideal for chasing Killer Croc. Like all hovercraft, it can skim over water or land on a cushion of air, and is powered by large propellers. Unlike other hovercraft, it also has a pair of cool bat-shaped wings!

TWO-FACE
DON'T GET ON HIS BAD SIDE!

VITAL STATS
....

LIKES: Playing heads or tails
DISLIKES: Matching outfits
FRIENDS: His other half
FOES: Batman
SKILLS: Seeing things from both sides
GEAR: Machine gun, lucky coin

SET NAMES: The Batmobile: Two-Face's Escape
SET NUMBERS: 7781
YEARS: 2006

Unruly hair on left-hand side of head.

Purple facial scarring only covers left-hand side of face.

White suit on dark-haired side... and dark suit on white-haired side!

SPLITTING HAIRS

Two-Face was the first LEGO minifigure to have multicoloured hair – made from white plastic with black printing. Poison Ivy and Wonder Woman also have printing on their hair pieces.

Lots of people in Gotham City lead double lives, but Two-Face takes it to extremes! One of the city's biggest crime bosses, he is in two minds about everything and makes decisions by flipping his lucky coin – unlucky for some!

TWO-FACE'S HENCHMAN
BANDED BANDIT

VITAL STATS
....

LIKES: Black and white
DISLIKES: Sorting laundry
FRIENDS: Two-Face's
right side
FOES: Two-Face's wrong
side... or is it the other
way around?
SKILLS: Bank robbery
GEAR: Handgun

SET NAMES: The Batmobile:
Two-Face's Escape
SET NUMBERS: 7781
YEARS: 2006

Black and white
scheme echoes
Two-Face's suit.

Black
handgun

HEELS ON WHEELS
The bank truck hijacked by
Two-Face and his Henchman
boasts an armoured windshield,
a booby-trapped roof and
hidden weapons that fold
out from the sides.

What's black and white and green
all over? A stolen Gotham City Bank
truck filled with banknotes and
Two-Face's goon! This Henchman
is always happy to help out with a
bank heist – although you wouldn't
know it from the look on his face!

23

THE JOKER
THE CLOWN PRINCE OF CRIME

VITAL STATS
....

LIKES: Practical jokes
DISLIKES: Brushing his teeth
FRIENDS: Henchman
FOES: Batman and Robin
SKILLS: Madcap scheming
GEAR: Gag gun

SET NAMES: The Batwing:
The Joker's Aerial Assault,
The Tumbler: Joker's Ice
Cream Surprise
SET NUMBERS: 7782, 7888
YEARS: 2006, 2008

Unique green
hair piece with
pointed edges

Laughter lines
around eyes and
mouth from too
much grinning.

Don't sniff the
flower – it spits acid!

FUN IN THE GUN
The Joker's armoury of
outlandish weapons ranges
from the silly to the scary. One
of his favourites is a gun that
fires a flag with the word
"BANG!" written on it.

BANG!

This clownish character is no
fool – he's the prince of crime in
Gotham City! His grin hides a deep
hatred of Batman and Robin, and
his jokes always have a sting in the
tail. He is out to cause chaos at
every comic turn!

THE JOKER'S HENCHMAN
WILL WORK FOR SNACKS

VITAL STATS
....

LIKES: Ice lollies
DISLIKES: Brain freeze
FRIENDS: The Joker,
Mr Freeze
FOES: Batman and Robin
SKILLS: Flying the Joker's
helicopter
GEAR: Nice hat

SET NAMES: The Batwing:
The Joker's Aerial Assault,
The Tumbler: Joker's Ice
Cream Surprise
SET NUMBERS: 7782, 7888
YEARS: 2006, 2008

Purple top matches
the Joker's jacket

Classic henchman hat

Ice lolly from the
Joker's Ice-Cream Van

IT'S THAT MAN AGAIN
A familiar-looking Henchman
also assists Mr Freeze in The
Batcave: The Penguin and Mr
Freeze's Invasion (set 7783).
He wears a blue top and black
gloves along with his usual hat.

The Joker's Henchman looks
remarkably like Two-Face's
Henchman (p.23). Perhaps he is the
same hired hand, prepared to do
the dirty work for whoever keeps
him stocked up with sunglasses
and knitted hats – or ice lollies!

25

THE JOKER COPTER
SKY-HIGH SURPRISE

The Joker's Henchman is at the controls!

VITAL STATS
....

OWNED BY: The Joker
USED FOR: Dropping laughing gas on Gotham
GEAR: Missiles, gas bombs

SET NAMES: The Batwing: The Joker's Aerial Assault
SET NUMBERS: 7782
YEARS: 2006

Copter sides fold down to reveal missiles

BOMBS AWAY
Pulling the rod at the back of the Copter releases grinning green gas bombs from a hidden compartment. The Joker also likes to throw these while hanging from the rope ladder!

Detachable rope ladder held in place with LEGO® Technic pin

This helicopter looks harmless — until its sides fold down to reveal hidden weapons! Part of the Joker's plan to cover Gotham City with toxic laughing gas, it can also use its side-mounted satellite dish to deflect missiles from Batman's Batwing.

THE JOKER'S ICE CREAM TRUCK
THE CHILLING JOKE

VITAL STATS
••••••••••••••••••••••••••••

OWNED BY: The Joker
USED FOR: Selling Joker-gas ice creams
GEAR: Missile launcher

SET NAMES: The Tumbler: Joker's Ice Cream Surprise
SET NUMBERS: 7888
YEARS: 2008

Missile launcher disguised within giant multi-coloured ice-cream scoops

Logo promises a surprise – but not a nice one!

Spring-loaded missile

NOT-SO-NICE CREAM

Three very unpleasant sounding flavours of ice cream are listed on the back of the Joker's truck: Soda Smile Pop Sickle, Ol' Fashioned Venom Flavor, and Rigor Mortis Soft Ice!

Venom for making toxic ice creams goes inside slots labelled "venom".

Registration plate reads "I Scream".

The colourful cone on top of this truck isn't just for show, it's also a lever that fires a giant missile out through the back doors! The Joker will need this secret weapon when Batman hears about his tasteless plan to sell toxic gas ice creams.

BATWING
A SYMBOL OF HOPE

VITAL STATS
....

OWNER: Batman
USED FOR: Aerial battles
GEAR: Missile
launcher, rockets

SET NAME: The Batwing:
The Joker's Aerial Assault
SET NUMBER: 7782
YEAR: 2006

Missile launcher
folds away into tail

Missile
in flight

Back wings lift
to reveal
rockets

LANDING GEAR
The Batwing has its own landing
bay in the Batcave, with a
folding ladder that leads to the
cockpit. It is always ready for
vertical take-off, straight up
into the sky.

Forward prongs
can snare enemies
in mid-air

If Gotham City comes under
attack from the air, Batman takes
to the skies in this special fighter
jet. It is shaped like the bat-
symbol, so that the citizens below
can look up and see that the Caped
Crusader is on the case.

BATCOPTER
FLYING WITHOUT WINGS

VITAL STATS

....

OWNER: Batman
USED FOR: Patrolling the skies
GEAR: Lasers, rockets, missile

SET NAME: The Batcopter: The Chase for Scarecrow
SET NUMBER: 7786
YEAR: 2007

Rotor blades fold up when not in use

Targeting display

Air-to-air missile

Jet fuel goes in here

Twin laser cannons

CROW VS. BAT

When Batman battles the Scarecrow, he needs a biplane-busting missile to stop the raggedy wrongdoer from dropping fear-gas bombs on the people below!

Like the Batwing (opposite), this high-tech helicopter can take off and land vertically, without the need for a runway. It can also hover in one place in mid-air, making it useful for Batman's escapes and rescue missions.

THE PENGUIN
FREE AS A BIRD

VITAL STATS

LIKES: Sharp tailoring
DISLIKES: Prison jumpsuits
FRIENDS: The Arkham Asylum inmates
FOES: Batman and Robin
SKILLS: Operating riotous rides
GEAR: Umbrella, fish, gun

SET NAMES: Batman: Arkham Asylum Breakout, Jokerland
SET NUMBERS: 10937, 76035
YEARS: 2013, 2015

DID YOU KNOW?
The original 2006 Penguin minifigure didn't have an eye showing through his monocle.

Monocle

Umbrella doubles as a weapon

Purple mini-legs

DRESSED TO IMPRESS
Batman's oldest foe, the Penguin fancies himself as an upstanding Gotham City citizen. Always impeccably dressed, the original 2006 Penguin minifigure wore an elegant tuxedo with an orange waistcoat in sets 7783 and 7885.

Giggling gangster Oswald Cobblepot loves waddling off with other people's riches. The fowl fiend is no featherbrain, although he keeps his secrets safely under his top hat, and is never far from one of his gadget-laden umbrellas.

THE PENGUIN SUBMARINE
SWIMMING WITH THE FISHES

VITAL STATS

OWNER: The Penguin
USED FOR: Jewel theft
GEAR: Missiles fore and aft

SET NAME: Robin's Scuba
Jet: Attack of The Penguin
SET NUMBER: 7885
YEAR: 2008

Torpedo
launcher

Periscope for
seeing what's
going on above
water

Tower section
lifts off

Intimidating
Penguin face
on prow

Lever fires a
missile from
the stern

GOING UNDERGROUND

With Mr Freeze on board, the
Penguin sets course for
Batman's secret base in The
Batcave: The Penguin and
Mr Freeze's Invasion (set
7783). This earlier sub is
labelled U98 on the side.

The Penguin's tally
of Bat battles!

Numbered U99 (the "U" stands
for "undersea"), this sub swims as
well as a real seabird! On the hull,
the Penguin has marked the fact
that he has fought four battles
with Batman, and is now hoping to
get away with a stolen crystal!

31

MR FREEZE
COLD-HEARTED SCIENTIST

VITAL STATS

LIKES: Just chillin'
DISLIKES: Hot tubs
FRIENDS: The Penguin
FOES: Batman and Robin
SKILLS: Freezing things
GEAR: Freeze ray, armour

SET NAMES: The Batcave: The Penguin and Mr Freeze's Invasion, Batman's Buggy: The Escape of Mr Freeze
SET NUMBERS: 7783, 7884
YEARS: 2006, 2008

Goggles worn over eyes that are capable of producing icy blasts

Helmet keeps this criminal cool

STONE COLD STEAL
Mr Freeze wields a different ray gun as he makes his getaway from a diamond robbery. Driving a sub-zero speedster, he hopes to freeze Batman's pursuing Buggy in its tracks!

Freeze ray puts enemies on ice

Backpack pumps coolant round suit

A lab accident permanently lowered Dr Victor Fries' body temperature, forcing him to wear a special suit of armour at all times. Now calling himself Mr Freeze, he turned to crime to fund his scientific research.

POISON IVY
NAUGHTY BY NATURE

VITAL STATS

LIKES: Plants and flowers
DISLIKES: Pesticides
FRIENDS: Bane
FOES: Batman and Robin
SKILLS: Biology, plant control
GEAR: Twisted vines

SET NAMES: The Batcave, Batman: Arkham Asylum Breakout, Jokerland
SET NUMBERS: 6860, 10937, 76035
YEARS: 2012, 2013, 2015

Leaves curl through Ivy's flaming red hair.

A kiss from these sly lips will soon make you snooze.

THE ECO-WARRIOR

The 2006 Poison Ivy minifigure had exclusive dark red hair, green lips and black eyes with light green eye shadow. Although a brilliant botanist, she would still love to escape her greenhouse-styled prison in Arkham Asylum (set 7785).

Poison Ivy's leafy costume is also printed on the back.

As twisted as her beloved vines, Poison Ivy just wants to save the environment – from the human race. Able to control plants by the power of her mind, Ivy is immune to all poisons. Just don't let her pucker up for a kiss!

THE SCARECROW
MASTER OF FEAR

Wide-brimmed scarecrow hat

Scary cloth face

Rope fashion accessories

His tattered clothing is also printed on the back of the minifigure.

LIVING NIGHTMARE
Luckily, Scarecrow doesn't have Nyctophobia, fear of the dark, or Cleithrophobia, fear of being locked up, as he spends lots of time in jail. Not that it would matter, as his earlier 2006 minifigure, in set 7786, had a glow-in-the-dark head!

Shunned by his friends and family, phobia expert Dr Jonathan Crane decided to terrify everyone in Gotham City. As the Scarecrow, he uses his homemade fear gas to bring his victims' worst nightmares to life.

SCARECROW'S BIPLANE
AS THE CROW FLIES

VITAL STATS

OWNER: Scarecrow
USED FOR: Fear gas attacks
GEAR: Fear gas bombs,
machine guns

SET NAME: The Batcopter:
The Chase for Scarecrow
SET NUMBER: 7786
YEAR: 2007

Biplanes take their name from having two sets of wings.

Scarecrow holds onto his scythe while flying

Scary scarecrow face on tail fin

GREEN FEAR GAS BOMBS

As well as having two tanks of fear gas ready to spray, Scarecrow's Biplane is also equipped with fear gas bombs. Coloured the same ghastly green, they have horrible grinning pumpkin heads inside!

Spinning propeller

One of four machine guns

Scarecrow scythes through the sky in his biplane. It might look old-fashioned, but its four machine guns are very high-tech: perfectly placed to fire between moving rotor blades. Plus it carries weapons that are the cutting-edge of criminal chemistry!

THE RIDDLER
GOTHAM CITY'S CLUED-UP CRIMINAL

VITAL STATS

LIKES: Dangling sidekicks from cranes
DISLIKES: Straight talking
FRIENDS: The Joker, Harley Quinn
FOES: Batman and Robin
SKILLS: Creating riddles
GEAR: Question-mark cane

SET NAMES: The Dynamic Duo Funhouse Escape
SET NUMBERS: 6857
YEARS: 2012

DID YOU KNOW?
The Dynamic Duo Funhouse Escape set includes a mini-Riddler mannequin in the ticket office.

The 2012 Riddler minifigure now wears a bowler hat in place of black hair.

Defined muscles show through green suit.

There's no question about the Ridder's favorite punctuation mark!

CARRIED AWAY
In 2006, the Riddler was carted off to Arkham Asylum (set 7785) sporting a shock of black hair and a slightly simpler green outift. This variant also cropped up in The Bat-Tank: The Riddler and Bane's Hideout (set 7787).

One of Gotham City's most confusing villains, Edward Nygma likes to leave a trail of cryptic clues to help Batman foil his crimes. No one knows why. It's a complete mystery, and the most puzzling of all of the Riddler's riddles.

BAT-TANK
CAN'T BE STOPPED IN ITS TRACKS!

VITAL STATS
....

OWNER: Batman
USED FOR: Going where other land vehicles can't go
GEAR: Missiles, rockets

SET NAMES: The Bat-Tank: The Riddler and Bane's Hideout
SET NUMBERS: 7787
YEARS: 2007

Batman is well protected lying down inside the Bat-Tank

DID YOU KNOW?
Batman has more than 10 different Batmobiles, but only one Bat-Tank!

Triple missile launcher comes with yellow side missiles and a rubber-nosed rocket.

ENTER THROUGH GATE
The bunker-busting Bat-Tank has no problem breaking in to Bane's fortified hideout, easily knocking down the chained-up gates that come with this set.

Caterpillar tracks turn on inner wheels

What's a Super Hero to do when he already owns cars, motorcycles, boats, planes and helicopters? Get a tank, of course! Batman's Bat-Tank has huge tracks for crawling over tough terrain and a weapons turret with two types of missile.

HARLEY QUINN
DIAMOND DEVIANT

VITAL STATS
LIKES: Rollercoasters
DISLIKES: Heroic characters
FRIENDS: The Joker,
the Riddler
FOES: Batman and Robin
SKILLS: Setting traps
GEAR: Rollercoaster car

SET NAMES: The Dynamic
Duo Funhouse Escape
SET NUMBERS: 6857
YEARS: 2012

Harley Quinn was the first LEGO minifigure to wear a jester's hat.

A revolving head reveals a mischievous grin.

The red and black card game colour scheme continues with diamond motifs.

ARMED TO THE TEETH
The 2008 Harley Quinn from set 7886 had a wide, manic grin, but had not yet learnt good dental care – her teeth were stained a horrible yellow colour! Mocking her looks, however, is not advised, as she's equipped with not one, but two, weapons!

Harleen Quinzel was the Joker's doctor at Arkham Asylum, but instead of curing her criminal patient, she joined him on a crazy crime spree as Harley Quinn. Now, she has fun causing chaos in Gotham City with her beloved puddin' Mr J!

HARLEY'S HAMMER TRUCK
MANIC MOTOR

Harley's minifigure holds yet another hammer.

VITAL STATS
....

OWNER: Harley Quinn
USED FOR: Flattening foes
GEAR: Giant hammer, rocket launchers

SET NAMES: The Batcycle: Harley Quinn's Hammer Truck
SET NUMBERS: 7886
YEARS: 2008

"WHACK-A-BAT" scrawled on hammer

HAMMER TIME
Batman rides a winged Batcycle in pursuit of Harley's Hammer Truck. Both his armour and the motorcycle have the same flat-topped bat-symbol up front.

Monster-truck wheels

Look out: Harley Quinn is hitting the streets – literally! Her mashing machine has a huge mechanical hammer to whack anything in its path. Batman had better move fast to stop her giving his Batcycle a flat tyre – and a flat everything else!

39

BANE
BRAWN AND BRAINS COMBINED

VITAL STATS

LIKES: Strength-giving Venom
DISLIKES: Prisons
FRIENDS: Poison Ivy
FOES: Batman and Robin
SKILLS: Genius-level intelligence
GEAR: Mole machine

SET NAMES: The Batcave
SET NUMBERS: 6860
YEARS: 2012

Head encased in a mask so Bane can constantly breathe in Venom.

Artificially developed muscles

No gloves: Bane likes to break things with his bare hands.

THREE-WHEELING

Similar in dress apart from his blue trousers and slightly different head mask, the 2007 Bane still looks tough and brutish. He patrols his hideout in set 7787 on a three-wheeled dirt bike equipped with a missile launcher and a sidecar with a laser weapon.

Don't be fooled by all those muscles, super-villain Bane is no meathead. Able to speak dozens of different languages, this menacing mastermind uses a serum known as Venom to give himself super-strength and agility.

THE TUMBLER
READY TO RUMBLE

OWNER: Batman
USED FOR: Patrolling the mean streets of Gotham City
GEAR: Missiles, cannon

SET NAME: The Tumbler: Joker's Ice Cream Surprise
SET NUMBER: 7888
YEAR: 2008

Rear missiles hide beneath the Tumbler's sharp angles.

DID YOU KNOW?
The Tumbler was originally designed to leap across rivers and deploy bridges linking one side to the other.

Raised fins assist braking

Smaller front wheels for tight turns

SECRET WEAPON
The back of the Tumbler has a hidden launcher that flips up to fire a large rubber-tipped missile. The missile can be locked in place with a LEGO® Technic pin.

Twin machine guns lie between the front wheels

This angular assault vehicle is heavily armed with two different types of missile. The cockpit has room for Batman and a passenger (or a handcuffed prisoner!), and four extra-large back wheels power the vehicle into battle.

BATMAN
CLASSIC-STYLE CAPED CRUSADER

VITAL STATS

LIKES: Rescue missions
DISLIKES: Terrible traps
FRIENDS: Robin
FOES: The Joker, the Riddler, Harley Quinn
SKILLS: Motorcycle stunts
GEAR: Batarangs, Batmobile

SET NAMES: The Dynamic Duo Funhouse Escape, The Batcave
SET NUMBERS: 6857, 6860
YEARS: 2012

Batman's eyes cannot be seen through his suit's cowl.

Fabric cloak for dramatic poses.

Batman's trusty Batarang has appeared in more than 20 LEGO sets.

Classic bat-symbol on a bright yellow disc.

Gadgets can be attached to Utility Belt.

SPREADING HIS WINGS

To stop Catwoman from making a purr-fect getaway, Batman swaps his cape for glider wings and a jetpack to take to the air and chase after her in Catwoman Catcycle City Chase (set 6858).

Heroic Batman dons this classic comic book colour scheme to free Robin from a fiendish funfair. His blue and grey suit is more than enough to strike terror into Gotham's super-villain community.

THE JOKER
STILL THINKS HE'S FUNNY

VITAL STATS
....

LIKES: A good laugh
DISLIKES: Arkham Asylum
FRIENDS: Harley Quinn
FOES: Batman and Robin
SKILLS: Chemistry
GEAR: Remote control

SET NAMES: Dynamic Duo's
Funhouse Escape, Batwing
Battle over Gotham City,
Batman: Defend the Batcave,
The Joker Bumper Car
SET NUMBERS: 6857,
6863, 10672, 30303
YEARS: 2012, 2013,
2014, 2015

Yellow teeth revealed in wide grin on one side of head.

New waistcoat design features a lurid lime-green pattern.

BEHIND THE SMILE
The Joker's manic laughter hides
a keen intelligence. His fiendish
plots are full of surprises, which
is why a spin of this minifigure's
head reveals a sneaky smirk.

Remote control for Joker's latest barmy bat-trap!

Still mad, bad and dangerous to
know, the Joker is up to his same, old
tricks. With a yellow grin stretched
across the chalk-white face of this
minifigure variant, Batman's greatest
enemy is about to launch his own
brand of toxic laughing gas.

BRUCE WAYNE
CRIME-FIGHTING BILLIONAIRE

VITAL STATS

LIKES: The Batcave
DISLIKES: Drill tanks
FRIENDS: Robin
FOES: Poison Ivy, Bane
SKILLS: A quick change
GEAR: Bat-phone

SET NAME: The Batcave
SET NUMBER: 6860
YEAR: 2012

DID YOU KNOW?
Bruce's stern expression is similar to the face you'll find under the Batman minifigure's cowl.

Slicked-back black hair

Chiseled cheekbones and a serious expression

A stylish sand-blue suit

THE CALL TO ACTION
Bruce knows about trouble as soon as the phone rings. Luckily, the elevator is ready to transform him into Batman and drop him into the fight!

BAT-GEAR

Billionaire Bruce Wayne puts his vast riches to good use fighting crime as Batman, and yet his worse nightmares come true when Bane drills into the top-secret Batcave. Bruce doesn't want anyone to discover his secret identity.

ROBIN
OLDER BOY WONDER

VITAL STATS
LIKES: Using his brains
DISLIKES: Being treated like a child
FRIENDS: Batman
FOES: The Joker
SKILLS: Detecting
GEAR: Grappling hook

SET NAMES: The Dynamic Duo Funhouse Escape, The Batcave, Robin and the Redbird Cycle
SET NUMBERS: 6857, 6860, 30166
YEARS: 2012, 2012, 2013

Robin's head swivels to reveal a shocked expression for when facing the scariest of villains.

DID YOU KNOW?
Several people have fought crime in the guise of Robin, including Dick Grayson, Tim Drake and Damian Wayne.

Fabric cape similar to Batman's

BOY GENIUS AT WORK
Tim Drake is known as the Boy Wonder for a reason! He is a first-class scientist and engineer and he can use the Batcomputer as well as Batman himself – maybe even better!

Utility Belt pouches hold everything a top sidekick needs!

Stepping out on his own, but still fighting crime as Robin, Tim Drake donned a more serious, all-red costume. The single colour makes it look like Tim no longer has time for fun, and certainly this variant does not feature a smiling expression.

BATCYCLE
RIDING TO THE RESCUE

VITAL STATS

OWNER: Batman
USED FOR: Rapid rescues
GEAR: Rocket boosters

SET NAMES: The Dynamic Duo Funhouse Escape
SET NUMBERS: 6857
YEARS: 2012

Adjustable handlebars

DID YOU KNOW?
There have been three different LEGO Batcycles so far, as well as two-wheelers for Nightwing, Catwoman, and Bane.

Extra grip provided by chunky wheels

Rocket exhaust for bursts of speed

ON TRACK
The Joker's funhouse includes a rollercoaster cart in colours matching Harley Quinn's costume. To date, it is the only LEGO DC Comics Super Heroes vehicle to run on tracks.

Batman uses this Batcycle to race to the rescue when the Riddler, the Joker, and Harley Quinn team up to trap Robin inside a funhouse filled with twisted traps! Its slim shape is perfect for dodging whatever the villains can throw at him.

BANE'S DRILL TANK
UNDERWORLD UNDERMINER

VITAL STATS
....

OWNER: Bane
USED FOR: Underground attacks
GEAR: Missile launchers, giant drill

SET NAMES: The Batcave
SET NUMBERS: 6860
YEARS: 2012

Lamp lights dark tunnels

Rotating drill carves through rock and earth

Missile ready to launch

BIKE STRIKEBACK

Inside the Batcave, Batman uses his Batcycle to take on Bane's Drill Tank. It is similar to the Batcycle in The Dynamic Duo Funhouse Escape (set 6857), but has yellow wheels and missile launchers.

Six wheels turn the caterpillar tracks

With its tunnel-boring machinery at the front, Bane's Drill Tank is primed to mine its way into the Batcave for a surprise attack on Batman and Robin! The armoured front also puts an impressive amount of space between the driver and his nemesis.

SUPERMAN
THE MAN OF STEEL

A determined face:
Superman is ready
to stand for truth
and justice.

Eye-catching
red cape

DEFENDER OF METROPOLIS

On the other side of his double-sided face, Superman wears a confident smile – the Kryptonian enjoys banishing alien threats from his hometown, Metropolis.

Superman's
yellow belt is
also printed
on his back.

The last survivor of the doomed planet Krypton, Superman was rocketed to Earth as a baby. Powered by the sun, the Man of Steel can fly faster than a speeding bullet, lift incredible weights and fire lasers from his eyes.

WONDER WOMAN
AMAZONIAN PRINCESS

The minifigure's hairpiece includes Wonder Woman's golden tiara.

Wonder Woman's costume is based upon the flag of the United States of America.

FORCING THE TRUTH
No one can lie once they're tangled in Wonder Woman's Lasso of Truth. A turn of her head shows how angry she was to be captured by Lex Luthor.

Born on Paradise Island, Amazonian Princess Diana trained to be a warrior from the moment she could fight. The strongest woman on the planet, she now fights crime as a member of the Justice League.

LEX LUTHOR
SUPERMAN'S GREATEST ENEMY

A serious face as Lex plots Superman's downfall.

No need for a hairpiece with this famously bald villain.

A sharp business suit to wear to work at his company—LexCorp.

EVIL GENIUS

A master inventor, Lex Luthor designed and built a Kryptonite-powered battle armour to defeat Superman once and for all. The bait in his trap? None other than Wonder Woman herself!

The Lex Luthor minifigure was the first LEGO DC Comics Super Heroes villain not to come from Batman's rogues gallery. Instead, powerful billionaire Lex Luthor is Superman's arch nemesis in the city of Metropolis.

POWER ARMOUR
LEX LUTHOR'S MEAN, GREEN MACHINE

VITAL STATS
....

OWNER: Lex Luthor
USED FOR: Setting a trap
for Superman
GEAR: Kryptonite gun

SET NAME: Superman vs
Power Armour Lex
SET NUMBER: 6862
YEAR: 2012

Pipe connects
gun to armour.

Clear dome protects
control seat.

Long gun barrel
channels Kryptonite
energy.

Wonder
Woman is
held in Lex's
clutches!

ALL FINGERS AND THUMBS

A LEGO® Technic pin holds
the gun in place on the
armour's right arm.
Both hands have
moveable thumbs and
two moveable fingers
that can grasp minifigures
and other objects.

Flexible joints
allow for giant
strides.

Lex Luthor grew one big,
mechanical step closer to catching
Superman with this Kryptonite-
powered robo-suit. Holding Wonder
Woman prisoner, he plans to lure
Superman into a trap and blast him
with the mech's Kryptonite gun.

LEX LUTHOR'S MECH

Superman vs Power Armour Mech (set 6862) allowed Lex Luthor to show off his technology skills in a big, green fighting machine. LEGO® Technic pins in the right arm turn his gun as he takes on two Super Heroes at once.

LEX LUTHOR
WICKED WARSUIT

VITAL STATS
....

LIKES: Kryptonite
DISLIKES: Red-caped heroes
FRIENDS: None
FOES: Superman
SKILLS: Great intelligence
GEAR: The Deconstructor

SET NAME: Lex Luthor
(polybag)
SET NUMBER: 30164
YEAR: 2012

This Luthor variant has a snarling face.

The warsuit follows Luthor's classic comic-book green and purple colour-scheme.

Rocket packs allow Lex to fly like Superman.

Remove the warsuit and you'll see a power-pack printed on the minifigure's chest.

FEAR THE DECONSTRUCTOR!

One of Luthor's most despicable weapons, the Deconstructor can pull apart any LEGO object made of black bricks. Luckily Superman's costume is blue and red. Phew!

DID YOU KNOW?
This exclusive Lex was given away at GameStop stores with pre-orders of LEGO *Batman 2: DC Super Heroes*.

Realising that he was physically no match for Superman, Lex designed a powerful new armour, capable of flight and boosting his strength to super-human levels. He really will do anything to bring down the Man of Steel.

BATMAN
ELECTRO SUIT SHOCKER

VITAL STATS
....

LIKES: Gotham City
DISLIKES: Law-breaking
FRIENDS: Robin
FOES: Gotham City's criminal community
SKILLS: Delivering electric shocks
GEAR: Electro suit

SET NAME: DK's LEGO *DC Universe™ Super Heroes Batman™ Visual Dictionary* Exclusive
SET NUMBER: N/A
YEAR: 2012

DID YOU KNOW?
The Electro suit made its first appearance in the LEGO *Batman 2: DC Super Heroes* video game.

No oval for the bat-symbol

A double-sided head also includes a smiling face on the other side.

POWER POINTS
Without a cape, the taser points on the back of Batman's minifigure are clearly visible. Bruce designed the suit to release charges from both the front and rear. What a clever spark!

Light blue lines show where electricity can be generated.

Taser points

Sometimes even Batman's martial arts aren't enough to bring down Gotham City's super-villains. The Dark Knight's Electro suit amps up the action by delivering an electric shock with every punch.

THE JOKER'S HENCHMAN
NO CLOWNING AROUND

VITAL STATS

LIKES: Being a grump
DISLIKES: Smiling
FRIENDS: The Joker
FOES: Batman
SKILLS: Helicopter pilot
GEAR: Laughing gas bomb

SET NAME: Batwing Battle Over Gotham City
SET NUMBER: 6863
YEAR: 2012

This henchman never fancies turning his frown upside down!

Lime green to match the Joker's waistcoat

Black gloves leave no fingerprints

BACK TO BASICS

There's no mistaking who this moaning minifigure works for. Not only are his clothes the Joker's trademark colours, but the Clown Prince of Crime's face is emblazoned on his back.

The Joker's henchman likes to crack safes but not smiles. This misery-guts is never happy. Maybe he doesn't like having his face painted. He'd better watch out, just in case the Joker gives him a dose of all that laughing gas!

THE JOKER'S HELICOPTER
TAKING A FUNNY TURN

VITAL STATS
....

OWNER: The Joker
USED FOR: Laughing-gas attacks
GEAR: Missiles, laughing-gas

SET NAME: Batwing Battle Over Gotham City
SET NUMBER: 6863
YEAR: 2012

DID YOU KNOW?
Set 6863 is an update of The Batwing: The Joker's Aerial Assault (set 7782) from 2006 (see p.26 and p.28).

"J" is for Joker

Toxic laughing-gas bomb

HA-HA-HANG ON!
The Joker loves to show off, and can't help swinging on a rope ladder with a joke-shop gun while his henchman is left with the serious job of controlling the chopper.

Launchers for missiles—one on each side

Uncharacteristically, there are big grins all round the Joker's Helicopter. Both sides show the Joker's own sinister smile, while the bomb at the front has a fearsome leer. Needless to say, it's filled with laughing gas!

BATWING
FLIGHT AND FIGHT

VITAL STATS

OWNER: Batman
USED FOR: Flying like a bat
GEAR: Homing missile, rocket launchers

SET NAMES: Batwing Battle Over Gotham City
SET NUMBERS: 6863
YEARS: 2012

Rear wings can tilt up and down.

Tail covers flaming exhaust

Front lights for night flying

BACK BUTTON

Flipping up the cover behind the cockpit reveals a hidden button. Pressing it launches a homing missile that has Batarang-like wings, which is docked on the underside of the vessel.

Wings echoes Bat-symbol shape

DID YOU KNOW?
The world's biggest bats can have wingspans of up to 170cm (5ft 6in).

Batman is ready to take on airborne enemies in his custom-built Batwing. It has rocket launchers hidden beneath its back wings and a homing missile under its tail, and is shaped like a bat so his opponents know who is coming for them!

BATMOBILE
GOOD LOOKS CATCH CROOKS!

VITAL STATS

OWNER: Batman
USED FOR: Fighting crime, looking cool
GEAR: Missiles

SET NAMES: Batmobile and the Two-Face Chase
SET NUMBERS: 6864
YEARS: 2012

Batwings protect rear engine from side-on attacks

Twin missile launchers

Cooling stacks

Plush red interior has room for Batman and his cape

Vents draw air into engine at rear

ARMS RACE

The Batmobile takes on a crane truck full of crooks when Two-Face and his henchmen raid a bank. Both cars fire super-fast missiles, but whose will hit their target first?

The sleek curves of the Batmobile hug the ground for a literal low profile – but the bright yellow wheels and flaming exhaust make for a pretty high-profile warning to crooks. Just one glimpse makes some of them quit crime altogether!

TWO-FACE
A MAN DIVIDED

Scarred face

Dynamite is ready to blow.

The original 2006 Two-Face minifigure used a LEGO stud as a coin, but this variant has a printed round tile.

MAKING HIS MIND UP
Two-Face made a bad decision when he stole a safe from Gotham City museum. Batman pursued and made sure the villain was soon laughing on the other side of his face.

Two-Face's split-colour suit continues on the back of his minifigure.

Talk about double-trouble.
Former District Attorney Harvey Dent still plans his crimes on the flip of his two-headed coin. This updated variant adds crazy colour to his originally black and white wardrobe.

GUARD
BRAVE BANK EMPLOYEE

VITAL STATS
....

LIKES: Standing guard
DISLIKES: Bank robbers
FRIENDS: Batman
FOES: Two-Face, henchmen
SKILLS: Brave and resourceful
GEAR: Walkie-talkie, handcuffs

SET NAMES: The Batmobile and The Two-Face Chase, Batman: Arkham Asylum Breakout
SET NUMBERS: 6860, 10937
YEARS: 2012, 2013

The Guard has the same face as the original 2006 Bruce Wayne minifigure.

LEGO handcuffs have appeared in more than 80 sets.

Guard uniform printing on torso.

EMPLOYEE OF THE YEAR

Because of his brave actions at the Bank, the guard was offered a job at Arkham Asylum. Keeping a bunch of criminals in their cells? All in a day's work!

ARKHAM ASYLUM

Most bank employees turned and ran when Two-Face raided Gotham City bank. Not this guard. He raised the alarm and called Batman personally, standing ready to handcuff Harvey Dent and his heinous henchmen.

TWO-FACE'S HENCHMAN ONE
HARVEY DENT'S RIGHT-HAND MAN

VITAL STATS

LIKES: Money
DISLIKES: Justice
FRIENDS: Two-Face, Henchman Two
FOES: Batman, the guard
SKILLS: Operating cranes
GEAR: Sunglasses

SET NAMES: The Batmobile and The Two-Face Chase
SET NUMBERS: 6864
YEARS: 2012

Cool shades: What every goon is wearing this season.

A similar colour scheme to his notorious boss.

Torso printed with zips and studs.

SAFE BREAK!

Henchman One only had one job on the raid on Gotham Bank – to make sure that the safe was safely hoisted clear. What a pity he forgot to shut the vault door!

From an early age, Henchman One knew he was destined to aid Gotham City's super-villains, and soon signed up to work with Two-Face. You can blame his mother. What kind of woman calls her son "Henchman One" anyway?

TWO-FACE'S HENCHMAN TWO
HARVEY DENT'S LEFT-HAND MAN

The mini pixie cap has appeared in more than 70 LEGO sets.

Villainous stubble and goatee combo.

Henchman Two wears the same jacket as his brother, Henchman One.

GETAWAY DRIVER

The one thing Henchman Two can do better than his brother is making a clean getaway – except for that time he left Two-Face's car in a "No Parking" zone and got it towed away.

Poor old Henchman Two has spent his entire life in the shadow of his older twin brother. Henchman Two came a sorry second in every class at goon school, including Tying Up Guards, Blowing Up Safes and Carrying Swag.

TWO-FACE'S CAR
IT'S GOT A DENT IN IT!

VITAL STATS

OWNER: Two-Face
USED FOR: Robbing banks
GEAR: Crane, missiles, machine gun

SET NAME: Batmobile and the Two-Face Chase
SET NUMBER: 6864
YEAR: 2012

Bullet holes decorate car hood and crane

Two-Face stands at the crane controls.

Stolen bank safe opens to reveal loot

Launcher for two missiles

Machine gun made from four LEGO binoculars pieces

IT'S A STEAL!
The Batmobile and the Two-Face Chase set includes a bank building with a lever to knock out its windows, making it easy for Two-Face's crane to snatch the safe!

Harvey Dent, aka Two–Face, is causing trouble in his colourful crane car. Making his getaway after a bank robbery, he hopes some witnesses will say they saw a purple car leaving the scene, while others will swear it was orange!

BIZARRO
SUPERMAN IN REVERSE

VITAL STATS

LIKES: Being bad
DISLIKES: Clark Kent
FRIENDS: The Bizarro League
FOES: Superman
SKILLS: Freezing vision and flaming breath
GEAR: Purple-blue flying cape

SET NAME: Bizarro
SET NUMBER: COMCON022
YEAR: 2012

DID YOU KNOW?
In LEGO *Batman 3: Beyond Gotham* Bizarro stole Luthor's duplication ray to make Bizarro versions of the Justice League.

Chalk white and wrinkled skin

Reversed S-shield and muted colours

A medallion made of rock helps Bizarro remember his own name.

BIZARRO BOTHER
The other side of Bizarro's head shows an even angrier face. The mixed-up minifigure was a San Diego Comic-Con exclusive, only available at the convention.

Created by evil genius Lex Luthor, this muddled clone of Superman gets everything the wrong way around. Childish and prone to throwing tantrums, Bizarro sees life in reverse. For him, good is bad and bad is good.

65

SHAZAM!
THE WORLD'S MIGHTIEST MORTAL

VITAL STATS

LIKES: Being a hero
DISLIKES: Being a kid
FRIENDS: The Justice League
FOES: Black Adam
SKILLS: Magical abilities
GEAR: White cape

SET NAME: Shazam
(SDCC 2012 exclusive)
SET NUMBER: COMCON020
YEAR: 2012

DID YOU KNOW?

Shazam appears in the LEGO *Batman 2: DC Comics Super Heroes* and LEGO *Batman 3: Beyond Gotham* video games.

Shazam shares a hairpiece with Bruce Wayne.

Printed body emblazoned with lightning strike

Shazam wears one of the longest capes to appear on a LEGO DC Comics Super Heroes minifigure.

RAGE AND FURY

Shazam uses his great wisdom to think his way out of trouble. That doesn't means he always remains calm. The other side of Shazam's head shows him shouting in anger.

Aged ten, Billy Batson was granted magical powers by a wizard. By shouting "Shazam!" Billy changes into a powerful being blessed with the ability of legendary heroes Solomon, Hercules, Atlas, Zeus, Achilles and Mercury (spelling "Shazam").

JOR-EL
SUPERMAN'S FATHER

VITAL STATS

LIKES: Science
DISLIKES: The Kryptonian Council
FRIENDS: His wife Lara
FOES: General Zod
SKILLS: Code imprinting
GEAR: Dark brown cape

SET NAME: Jor-El (polybag)
SET NUMBER: 5001623
YEAR: 2013

DID YOU KNOW?

This minifigure is based on the 2013 *Man of Steel* movie. It was given free to customers at shop.LEGO.com and LEGO stores in June 2013.

Armour detailing is similar to Superman's *Man of Steel* variant

The "S" symbol means "hope" in Kryptonian.

FROM FATHER TO SON

As "Clark Kent", Superman discovered a Kryptonian spaceship on Earth. From it, a holographic image of Jor-El appeared to teach Clark about his alien heritage and present the Last Son of Krypton with his Superman uniform.

While Superman's armour is gold in tones, Jor-El's is bronze.

When chief scientist Jor-El realized that his planet Krypton was about to explode, he tried to warn the Kryptonian High Council. With Jor-El's advice going ignored, he sent his son to Earth for safety. This son would become Superman!

GREEN ARROW
THE EMERALD ARCHER

VITAL STATS
....

LIKES: Hitting the bull's-eye
DISLIKES: Commitment
FRIENDS: The Justice League
FOES: Merlyn
SKILLS: Archery
GEAR: Green hood

SET NAME: Green Arrow
(SDCC 2013 exclusive)
SET NUMBER: COMCON030
YEAR: 2013

Green hood

DID YOU KNOW?
This is the only LEGO DC Comics Super Heroes Green Arrow minifigure not to have a bow and arrow!

Cool Super Hero stubble

Arrow insignia on belt

TWO'S COMPANY
This rare Green Arrow kept company with black-suited Superman (see p.85) at the 2013 San Diego Comic-Con.

Kneepads printed on legs

Another Comic-Con exclusive, 200 Green Arrow minifigures were offered up for raffle in July 2013. They are based on Green Arrow's updated 2011 costume from the comics. Previously, Green Arrow had sported a yellow goatee.

WINGED BATMAN
SWOOPING SUPER HERO

Costume is now
black rather than
blue and grey

COWL SPOTTER
Batman has worn three moulded
LEGO cowls. Early minifigures
wore type one cowl (left) before
it was swapped for the more
curved type two (right). A third
cowl was introduced in 2015.

Plastic wings replace
usual fabric cape for
an exclusive one-set
appearance.

Utility Belt
now contains
pockets

This Batman also appears, without
his wings, in Batman Jetski (3016),
Super Secret Police Dropship (70815),
Batman: Man-Bat Attack (76011),
The Batmobile and the Two-Face
Chase (6864) and Batman: The
Joker Steam Roller (76013) sets.

THE JOKER
ARKHAM PRISONER

The back of the minifigure is printed with Joker's Arkham Asylum inmate number – 109370!

Same hair as the regular Joker variant

Bright orange Arkham jumpsuit

PARTNERS IN CRIME

The doctors at Arkham Asylum hoped they could prepare the Joker for civilised law-abiding society, but the only thing the arch villain prepared behind bars were further crimes – especially with a certain Dr Harleen Quinzel!

Arkham Asylum is the Joker's home away from home, although he never stays for long. Batman thought he had the Clown Prince of Crime under lock and key, until the dastardly villain slipped his restraints in the Arkham security van.

DR HARLEEN QUINZEL
LAUGHTER IS THE BEST MEDICINE

VITAL STATS
....

LIKES: Gag weapons
DISLIKES: Unrequited love
FRIENDS: The Joker,
Poison Ivy
FOES: Batman and Robin
SKILLS: Escapology
GEAR: Jester's hat

SET NAME: Batman: Arkham
Asylum Breakout
SET NUMBER: 10937
YEAR: 2013

DID YOU KNOW?
Harley Quinn
first appeared in
a 1992 episode
of *Batman: The
Animated Series.*

A twist of Dr
Quinzel's head
reveals Harley
Quinn on the
other side!

Doctor's outfit
comes complete
with name
badge clipped
onto front.

Harley's costume
is peeking out
from beneath her
doctor's uniform.

MANIC MAKE-UP!
What every gal needs for a
quick change—Harleen has
a hidden make-up table at
Arkham, including a jester's hat
and a signed Joker pin-up!

No one knew that the Joker had
secretly persuaded psychiatrist
Harleen Quinzel to become the
villainous Harley Quinn. The double-
crossing doctor was then on hand to
help her puddin' to escape – along
with the rest of the inmates, too!

ROBIN
RED AND READY

DID YOU KNOW?
This minifigure is incredibly similar to the Robin in the *Batman: Arkham City* video game.

Hood to hide in the shadows

Two-sided head features a scared expression on the reverse.

Shorter cape worn for first time

Black gloves

BETTER THAN A BROLLY
The Penguin better watch out – Robin is armed and dangerous. The monocle-wearing menace may have more than a few tricks up his umbrella, but they're no match for Robin's kendo stick!

When Batman and Robin's greatest enemies escaped Arkham Asylum, the Boy Wonder began the long task of bringing them all back to justice. This hooded variant swapped Robin's usual red legs for black to remain hidden for longer!

SECURITY VAN
ALL ABOARD FOR ARKHAM

VITAL STATS

OWNER: Arkham Asylum
USED FOR: Prisoner transport
GEAR: Grill guard

SET NAME: Batman: Arkham Asylum Breakout
SET NUMBER: 10937
YEAR: 2012

Blue lights for use in an emergency

Room for one security guard

Arkham and Gotham City logos

IN THE BACK
Double doors at the back of the van are wide enough to take in a lying-down Joker, his restraining frame, and his broad, maniacal grin. He couldn't possibly escape. Could he?

Protective grill guard

This armoured vehicle serves as a prisoner transport for the most dangerous inmates of Arkham Asylum. The logo on the side lets citizens know they should steer clear, while blue lights on top flash as it speeds through the city!

ARKHAM ASYLUM

Batman revisits Arkham in Batman: Arkham Asylum Breakout (set 10937) when the Joker stages yet another jailbreak. A lot of grey bricks are required to complete this build!

THE JOKER? AGAIN?!

IT'S A NICE NIGHT FOR A BREAKOUT!

AQUAMAN
RULER OF ATLANTIS

VITAL STATS

LIKES: The ocean
DISLIKES: Ice prisons
FRIENDS: Batman
FOES: Mr Freeze
SKILLS: Controlling sea-life
GEAR: Golden trident

SET NAMES: Arctic Batman vs Mr Freeze: Aquaman on Ice, Black Manta Deep Sea Strike
SET NUMBERS: 76000, 76027
YEARS: 2013, 2015

An angry face as Aquaman plans a retaliation attack.

Aquaman can blast water out of his trident.

Aquaman's muscles are also printed on the back of the minifigure.

FROZEN FISH
The marine minifigure's reversible head shows a more somber expression. Aquaman had plenty of time to think when he was put on ice in Mr Freeze's petrifying polar prison.

Half-human and half-Atlantean, Aquaman tirelessly defends Earth's oceans from attack. The briny ruler is able to communicate telepathically with fish and sea mammals, and was one of the founding members of the Justice League.

ARCTIC BATBOAT
IN POLE POSITION

Batwing rudder
assists steering

BACK WITH A BANG
As well as fast-flying discs
launched from the front of
the vessel, the Arctic Batboat is
also armed with a pair of
ice-busting bombs at the back.

Targeting
computer display

Blades for skiing
over ice and
snow

Batman brings the heat in his
Arctic Batboat! Designed to
withstand the coldest conditions, it
cuts across ice and snow at speed.
That makes it the perfect rescue
craft when Aquaman gets frozen in
a block of ice by Mr Freeze.

ARCTIC BATMAN
A COLD KNIGHT

This minifigure uses the second version of Batman's LEGO cowl.

Bat-symbol in white and grey

White polar batsuit blends in with the snow.

A COLD SENSE OF HUMOR

Batman isn't always the warmest character, but a twist of the hero's head reveals a less frosty side. Even in icy conditions, the Dark Knight keeps his cool.

Available in just one LEGO set, Arctic Batman charges to the coldest place on Earth to rescue Aquaman from the chilly clutches of Mr Freeze. A camouflaged Caped Crusader will soon best the refrigerated rogue.

MR FREEZE
STILL AS COLD AS ICE

VITAL STATS
....

LIKES: Ice and snow
DISLIKES: Heat
FRIENDS: The Riddler
FOES: Batman, Aquaman
SKILLS: Cryogenics
GEAR: Freeze Gun

SET NAMES: Arctic
Batman vs Mr Freeze:
Aquaman on Ice
SET NUMBERS: 76000
YEARS: 2013

This minifigure variant's
face features an all-new
ferocious expression!

The Freeze Gun can
encase anyone in a
prison block of ice.

Air-conditioned wiring
beneath Mr Freeze's
armour keeps him
permanently chilled.

FREEZE GUN
Mr Freeze's 2013 Freeze
Gun combines a LEGO plate
piece with icy blue transparent
pieces for freezing action.
His bulky armour is suitably
high-tech to match.

Dr Victor Fries is as dangerous
as ever before, with bulkier armour
and an enhanced Freeze Gun.
Still seeking vengeance on those
he deems responsible for his frozen
condition, Mr Freeze thinks that
revenge is best served cold!

BATMAN
THE BANE OF BANE

Black cowl covers double-sided head

Sharp-edged bat-symbol

Printed body armour

Complex bronze Utility Belt

SAFE AND SOUND

Bane safely dispatched, Batman gives Gordon a lift back to police HQ in the Bat. Thanks to his alternative face, the Dark Knight looks happy to help out his old friend.

When this armoured Batman spots Bane chasing down Commissioner Gordon in a stolen Tumbler, he swoops to the rescue in the Bat. This set is inspired by the 2012 *The Dark Knight Rises* movie.

COMMISSIONER GORDON
CHIEF OF GOTHAM CITY POLICE

VITAL STATS
....

LIKES: Law and order
DISLIKES: Crime and deceit
FRIENDS: Batman
FOES: Bane
SKILLS: Keeping the peace
GEAR: Police handgun

SET NAME: The Bat vs Bane: Tumbler Chase
SET NUMBER: 76001
YEAR: 2013

Being a cop in Gotham City is a scary job!

SWAT stands for Special Weapons Attack Team.

Police issue firearm

SWAT'S GOING ON?
Gordon may look scared but a twist of his head reveals a calm, determined face. Years of being the Gotham City chief of police have taken their toll. Just look at those bags under Jim's eyes!

Can a bullet-proof vest *really* protect Gordon from villains like Bane?

Unlike most of the Gotham City police force, James Gordon is an honest cop. While Jim doesn't always approve of Batman's methods, he realises that the Dark Knight is Gotham City's last hope against dangerous super-villains like Bane.

BANE
ROAD HOG

Bane's mask is gone, revealing a shaved head and his breathing apparatus.

DID YOU KNOW?
This minifigure is inspired by Bane in *The Dark Knight Rises* movie of 2012.

Printing shows bulletproof vest

On one hand Bane wears a glove, on the other... he doesn't.

BULLETPROOF BACK
The back of Bane's 2013 minifigure shows more of his body armour while the straps that fix his breathing equipment to his bald head are clear.

Turning Batman's own weapons against him, Bane caused havoc as he tore up Gotham City's streets. Not even Jim Gordon's roadblocks could slow him down. The real question was whether Gordon could outrun this dangerous driver?

BANE'S TUMBLER
VILLAINOUS VEHICLE

VITAL STATS

OWNER: Bane (stolen from Wayne Enterprises)
USED FOR: Menacing Gotham City
GEAR: Armour plating, missile launchers

SET NAMES: The Bat vs Bane: Tumbler Chase
SET NUMBERS: 76001
YEARS: 2013

Hidden missile launchers

Bigger tyres at rear

Design echoes Bane's scary mask

UNDER THE ARMOUR

Flipping up the armour plating above the back wheels reveals the Tumbler's secret weapon: two hidden missile launchers! A hatch in the top also flips open to reveal Bane inside.

The first time Bruce Wayne saw a Tumbler, he had it painted black and turned it into his Batmobile. When thuggish Bane stole one for himself, he kept it in its original desert camouflage colours. Some villains just have no sense of style!

THE BAT
ARMED AND DANGEROUS

Click-joints
allow the
"arms" to
stay in
different
positions

Flick-fire missiles
on both arms

ROOM FOR ONE MORE
The Bat has a second seat in
the cockpit so that Gordon can
fit behind Batman when he's
finished hanging around.
Propellers ensure the pair
can speed away from Bane.

"Dark Knight"-
style bat-symbol

Gordon holds on
to the rescue rope

Batman chases after Bane and
comes to Gordon's rescue in this
experimental aircraft. Built by
Wayne Enterprises, it is powered
by propellers at the front and back,
and is equipped with cannons and
missiles on its two adjustable "arms".

SUPERMAN
THE MAN IN BLACK

DID YOU KNOW?
In the early 1990s, Superman wore a black costume with a chrome crest in the DC Comics books.

Distinctive curl

Silver S-Shield

Black outift signifies Superman's nightmare while captured in the Black Zero.

COSTUME CHANGE
This exclusive figure is actually a black and silver variant of the 2013 *Man of Steel* minifigure, which was released to tie into the movie of the same name.

It's the most somber Superman of all and also one of the rarest LEGO DC Comics Super Heroes minifigures. Superman in his black costume was given away to just 200 lucky raffle winners at San Diego Comic-Con on 20 July 2013.

LOIS LANE
DAILY PLANET REPORTER

VITAL STATS
....

LIKES: Following leads
DISLIKES: Being kidnapped
FRIENDS: Superman
FOES: General Zod
SKILLS: Investigating, escaping from aliens
GEAR: Wits and bravery

SET NAMES: Superman: Black Zero escape
SET NUMBERS: 76009
YEARS: 2013

DID YOU KNOW?
This Lois Lane minifigure is based on her appearance in the 2013 *Man of Steel* movie.

Lois shares her long red hair with eight other minifigures.

Exclusive head only available on this minifigure.

Printed blouse and waistcoat is suitable attire for a newshound.

ESCAPE POD PERIL
Is it any wonder the other side of Lois' head has a terrified expression? She's been thrown out of General Zod's Black Zero ship in an escape pod!

Practical blue trousers.

Intrepid reporter Lois Lane knew she had a story on her hands from the moment the first reports about Superman came in. Following her leads, she tracked the Man of Steel to his Smallville home and discovered his secret identity.

SUPERMAN
LAST SON OF KRYPTON

VITAL STATS

LIKES: Metropolis
DISLIKES: Falling structures
FRIENDS: Lois Lane, Jimmy Olsen
FOES: General Zod
SKILLS: Heat vision
GEAR: Red cape

SET NAMES: Superman: Metropolis Showdown, Superman: Battle of Smallville, Superman: Black Zero Escape
SET NUMBERS: 76002, 76003, 76009
YEAR: 2013

Peek beneath the cape and you'll see Superman's suit also printed on the back of the minifigure.

Silver armour detailing, as befits a battle-ready suit

TURNING UP THE HEAT
One side of Superman's head shows an angry expression and red eyes as he fights to save Metropolis and Smallville from the villainous Zod. The other side wears a calmer frown.

Details of the suit are also printed on the legs.

Darker than the classic Superman outfit, this more modern-looking Man of Steel has rid himself of the red pants over his tights. This suit is modelled on traditional Kryptonian clothing, worn under battle armour on Superman's home planet.

SPORTS CAR
METROPOLIS MOTOR

VITAL STATS
....

OWNER: Unknown
USED FOR: Kryptonian weightlifting
GEAR: Hot yellow paint job

SET NAME: Superman: Metropolis Showdown
SET NUMBER: 76002
YEAR: 2013

DID YOU KNOW?
The LEGO Group is the world's largest manufacturer of car tyres – although only very small ones!

Handles allow a minifigure to hold onto the car

NEED A LIFT?
This set also includes an antenna tower with a satellite dish, and a rubble ramp with a flip function to catapult the sports car – or the minifigures – into the air.

These tyres appear in more than 200 LEGO sets.

The car has room for a driver, but the set does not include one.

It's always a risk parking your car in Metropolis. You never know when a superpowered showdown is going to turn it into just another piece of junk to be thrown around. At least the driver of this sports car isn't inside when General Zod picks it up!

OFFROADER
BIG IN SMALLVILLE

VITAL STATS
....

OWNER: Colonel Hardy
USED FOR: Ground-to-air
defence
GEAR: Missile launcher

SET NAME: Superman: Battle
of Smallville
SET NUMBER: 76003
YEAR: 2013

DID YOU KNOW?
Brick-yellow
pieces such as the
Offroader's cabin,
were first seen in the
LEGO® Adventurers
theme in 1998.

Flick-fire
missiles

Rocket launcher
can rotate by
360 degrees

Cabin with
two seats is
one piece

HARDY DEFENCE
Brave Colonel Hardy knows his
Offroader's missile launcher
is no match for General
Zod's Black Zero
Dropship (p.94), but
he still uses it to
defend Smallville
when the Kryptonian
criminal attacks.

Chunky all-terrain tyres

This sand-coloured utility vehicle
is equipped for battle, with
searchlights and a pair of rocket
launchers mounted on the back. It
can seat two U.S. Air Force soldiers,
and is driven by Colonel Hardy when
Smallville comes under attack.

GENERAL ZOD
KRYPTONIAN CRIMINAL

VITAL STATS
....
LIKES: Making war
DISLIKES: The Phantom Zone
FRIENDS: Faora
FOES: Superman, Jor-El
SKILLS: Super-strength and speed
GEAR: Kryptonian helmet

SET NAMES: Superman: Battle of Smallville, Superman: Black Zero Escape
SET NUMBERS: 76003, 76009
YEAR: 2013

DID YOU KNOW?
A General Zod minifigure without his cape and helmet is available in Superman: Metropolis Showdown (set 76002).

Two-sided head featuring heat-vision eyes on the reverse

Black cape

General Zod's Kryptonian emblem

SPACE ARMOUR
Following Superman across the galaxy, Zod needs a Kryptonian battle helmet to breathe Earth's atmosphere. The aliens first clashed in the small town where Clark Kent, aka Superman, grew up – Smallville.

As the Planet Krypton ripped itself apart, Zod tried to overthrow the Kryptonian council and take control. Defeated, he and his co-conspirators were trapped in the Phantom Zone for all eternity – until Krypton's eventual destruction set them free!

COLONEL HARDY
U.S. AIR FORCE HERO

Bald head for
this bold hero

Pockets to
store ammo

Radio to call
for back up

DID YOU KNOW?
Colonel Hardy shares
a head with the Bank
Guard from The
Batmobile and the
Two-Face Chase
(set 8684).

GETTING ONE OVER GENERAL ZOD

Colonel Hardy becomes a hero
when he stages an attack on
Zod's spacecraft. He triggers a
portal that drags the ship back to
the Phantom Zone proving that
the mighty Dropship (see p.94) is
no match for the nifty offroader.

A member of the U.S. Air Force,
Colonel Nathan Hardy was ordered to
bring down the battling Kryptonians
that were flattening Smallville.
However, the Colonel realised that
the Man of Steel wasn't their enemy
after Superman saved his life.

FAORA
ZOD'S SECOND-IN-COMMAND

VITAL STATS

LIKES: Explosions
DISLIKES: Jor-El and his family
FRIENDS: General Zod,
Tor-An
FOES: Superman,
Colonel Hardy
SKILLS: Hand-to-hand
superpowered combat
GEAR: Helmet,
Kryptonian gun

SET NAME: Superman: Battle
of Smallville
SET NUMBER: 76003
YEAR: 2013

Shock! Faora shares a two-sided head with Wonder Woman!

Faora also shares hair with Nightwing and Beast Boy.

Faora's family crest

SOLAR-POWERED
Like Zod, Faora needs breathing apparatus to survive Earth's atmosphere, but she soon discovers that the solar system's yellow sun grants her new superpowers of her own. She won't be needing her gun!

Hips printed on the minifigure's body

To save Earth, Superman surrendered himself to Zod. The triumphant General sent his second in command, Faora, to collect the Man of Steel and Lois Lane. Their encounter would lead to a devastating battle in Smallville.

TOR-AN
KRYPTONIAN SOLDIER

VITAL STATS

LIKES: Fighting
DISLIKES: The Phantom Zone
FRIENDS: General Zod, Faora
FOES: Superman,
Colonel Hardy
SKILLS: Piloting the dropship
GEAR: Kryptonian gun

SET NAME: Superman: Battle
of Smallville
SET NUMBER: 76003
YEAR: 2013

DID YOU KNOW?
This minifigure has brown hair, just like his comic-book counterpart.

This minifigure has the same head as Lex Luthor.

Tor-An's Kryptonian emblem

No cape for this pilot – it would only restrict his space in the cockpit.

TOO BAD, TOR-AN
As the pilot of the dropship, Tor-An sees all of the action from his domed cockpit. After the battle on Earth, he is banished to the Phantom Zone by Colonel Hardy.

Tor-An helped General Zod track Superman's path through the cosmos to Earth. Genetically engineered to be a soldier and a loyal member of the Kryptonian Warrior Guild, Tor-An is a master of several alien martial arts.

BLACK ZERO DROPSHIP
ALIEN ATTACK CRAFT

Adjustable fins aid flight in atmosphere

Storage bays open to reveal weapons racks

Spring-loaded missiles hidden within hull

Rotating cannon fires crackling energy bolts

DROPPED SHIP
The Dropship is designed to land on planets, and its fins can fold down to become feet that keep the weapons array raised above the ground.

Criminal Kryptonians General Zod, Faora, and Tor-An set out to destroy the town of Smallville in this superpowered spaceship! Only Superman can stop them, but he will have to dodge giant missiles and blasts of alien energy to do so!

PLASTIC MAN
THE STRETCHABLE SUPER HERO

VITAL STATS
....

LIKES: Pranks, the
Justice League
DISLIKES: Being overstretched
FRIENDS: Batman
FOES: The Dart
SKILLS: Stretching into
any shape he wishes
GEAR: Groovy goggles

SET NAME: Plastic Man
(polybag)
SET NUMBER: 5004081
YEAR: 2014

Plastic Man
shares a
hairpiece with
Superman.

Those goggles
make Plastic Man
one cool dude –
or so he thinks!

A QUICK CHANGE

Plastic Man's costume is
also printed on the back. The
outfit was inspired by Plastic
Man's updated appearance
in the 2011 Flashpoint event.
This was Plastic Man's first
appearance with tights, instead
of bare legs.

Boots
printed
on legs

Given away at U.S. GameStop
stores with pre-orders of LEGO
Batman 3: Beyond Gotham, this
exclusive minifigure gave super-
stretchy Patrick "Eel" O'Brian a
fantastic plastic form. Plastic Man
has the power to reshape his body.

SMALLVILLE ATTACK
Superman faces new alien foes in Superman: Battle over Smallville (set 76003) in a new costume design to resemble his look from the 2013 *Man of Steel* movie.

THIS IS "HARDY" A WALK IN THE PARK, HARDY HAR HAR!

THE PENGUIN
WRAPPED UP WARM FOR WINTER

This variant still wears his monocle.

Newer umbrella has a brown handle.

Fur edging perfect for chilly crimes.

BIRD BRAINS
Constructed from simple LEGO bricks, these robot penguins stand guard around Penguin's stolen diamond. Their head design now comes with an attached bomb detonator, and the ice has turned their toes orange, rather than red (see p.16).

Talk about small man syndrome. The Penguin still has smaller than average legs, but he makes up for it with one of the biggest egos in Gotham City. With this new fur-lined coat, he's also the winner of the best dressed super-villain award!

SCUBA BATMAN
DEEP-SEA DETECTIVE

VITAL STATS
....

LIKES: Diving
DISLIKES: Jewel thieves
FRIENDS: Commissioner Gordon
FOES: The Penguin
SKILLS: First-class swimmer
GEAR: Scuba gear, harpoon

SET NAMES: Batman: The Penguin Face Off
SET NUMBERS: 76010
YEARS: 2014

Dark blue cowl accompanied by a scowl.

Harpoon gun at the ready.

Breathing apparatus leading to air tanks worn on the back.

Flippers for fast swimming action.

TAKE A DEEP BREATH
Scuba Batman's alternative face sees the Dark Knight wearing his breathing apparatus. The Penguin will be in hot water when Batman reels him in for stealing Gotham City's gems.

No villain is safe from Batman – not even on the water. This deep-sea variant is ready to dive straight into the deep end with unique scuba gear printing on his body. It's a good thing his gadgets are all waterproof!

THE PENGUIN DUCK BOAT
NOT JUST FOR SPLASHING ABOUT

Remote control operates robot penguins (see p.98)

VITAL STATS

OWNER: The Penguin
USED FOR: Brooding, hatching plans, bathtime
GEAR: Torpedo launchers

SET NAME: Batman: The Penguin Face Off
SET NUMBER: 76010
YEAR: 2014

Nice weather for ducks? Bring an umbrella!

Don't trust those big cute eyes...

Missiles hide under each wing (beneath the waterline)

DUCK TAIL

This duck doesn't have any legs to paddle with, so it needs a propeller at the back to power it. The Penguin controls the craft from the steering wheel inside.

Most people are content with a rubber ducky in their bathtub, but the Penguin takes fowl play to a whole new level! His bright yellow bird is big enough to ride in and rules its watery roost with two feather-ruffling rockets. Duck!

SCUBA VEHICLE
CHARTING NEW DEPTHS

VITAL STATS
....

OWNER: Batman
USED FOR: Diving
GEAR: Torpedo launchers

SET NAME: Batman: The
Penguin Face Off
SET NUMBER: 76010
YEAR: 2014

Batman in
scuba gear

Harpoon
gun

Clips to hold
harpoon

Torpedo
in flight

TWO BIRDS, ONE STONE
Batman uses his Scuba Vehicle
to find a stolen diamond that is
guarded by two of the Penguin's
robot helpers.

Fins steer left
and right

This solo speeder dives down
underwater so Batman can face his
fishiest foes. It is small enough not
to show up on enemy sensors, but
is still effective, thanks to its twin
torpedoes, powerful engine and
fishlike fins for steering.

NIGHTWING
BOY WONDER NO MORE

DID YOU KNOW?
Nightwing's new black and red costume first appeared in the DC Comics in 2013.

Double-sided head shows expressions of smiling or grim concentration.

Black gloves protect hands when using glider.

The "V" of Nightwing's insignia continues on the back of his top.

WINGED WONDER
Just like his mentor, Batman, Nightwing has plenty of cool vehicles. His rocket glider allows him to patrol the skies of Gotham City, keeping an eagle-eye out for trouble.

Acrobatic Dick Grayson enjoys the freedom of fighting crime on his own under the more grown-up identity of Nightwing. As a possible nod to the fact that he was once Robin, he changes his costume from blue to black and red. Neat!

MAN-BAT
GOTHAM CITY'S NIGHTMARE

Man-Bat's headpiece hides an alternative worried face.

Fur printing continues on the back as well as the chest of Man-Bat's minifigure.

Extended batwings move with arms.

GOING BATTY

Whenever Dr Langstrom transforms into Man-Bat, he becomes a wild beast capable of dropping dynamite on the unsuspecting heads of Gotham City's citizens.

When biologist friend of Bruce Wayne Dr Kirk Langstrom realised that he was going deaf, he created a serum that would give him the extraordinary hearing of bats. It worked, but also transformed him into a hideous bat-like monster!

BATCOPTER
A WHOLE NEW SPIN

VITAL STATS

OWNER: Batman
USED FOR: Pest control
GEAR: Missiles, winch

SET NAME: Batman:
Man-Bat Attack
SET NUMBER: 76011
YEAR: 2014

Missile in
launcher

Batwing-shaped
tail fin

Jet engines
on both sides

Missile in
flight

HOOKED!

Turning a gear at the
back of the Batcopter
lowers a hook on a rope.
Turning the gear the other
way reels in whatever – or
whoever – the winch
has hooked.

Flybars add
stability

Winch can snare
villains or
rescue friends

There's only room for one Bat
over Gotham City! So when the
monstrous Man-Bat launches an
aerial attack, Batman breaks out his
brilliant Batcopter. If its weapons
don't clip Man-Bat's wings, its
winch will bring him down to earth!

104

BATMOBILE
WHEN SPEED'S THE NEED

VITAL STATS
....

OWNER: Batman
USED FOR: Racing and chasing
GEAR: Hidden rockets

SET NAME: Batman: The Riddler Chase
SET NUMBER: 76012
YEAR: 2014

Twin exhausts

Adjustable rear wing for speed and defence

Downward-facing steering wheel

Bargeboards assist airflow for greater speed

POCKET ROCKETS

The back of the Batmobile has a hidden weapon. The entire rear section rises up above the cockpit to become a cannon ready to fire a pair of rockets!

DID YOU KNOW?
This Batmobile is inspired by the one that appears in the *Beware the Batman* animated series.

With its low, broad body and big, wide wheels, this Batmobile looks like a Formula 1 racing car. No wonder Batman uses it to keep up with his speedy Super Hero friend, The Flash – and with the villainous Riddler's own racing dragster.

BATMAN
BEWARE THIS BATMAN

VITAL STATS

LIKES: His new Batmobile
DISLIKES: Bombing along the road
FRIENDS: The Flash
FOES: The Riddler
SKILLS: Racing
GEAR: Batarang

SET NAME: Batman: The Riddler Chase
SET NUMBER: 76012
YEAR: 2014

DID YOU KNOW?

This outfit is based on the 2013 animated series Beware the Batman, complete with the show's distinctive bat-symbol.

Costume printing continues on the back

New style bat-symbol

New high-tech, bronzed Utility Belt has curvier edges than before.

FACING HIS ENEMIES

Batman may have a sleek new suit to go with a new Batmobile, but this minifigure still shares Batman's standard two-sided head from earlier variants, plus, of course, the trusty Batarang.

Grey gloves

Batman debuted a refined look as well as a new set of wheels when he had to take to the streets in a race against the Riddler. Time to buckle up with that shiny new Utility Belt and hit the road in the Batmobile!

THE FLASH
THE FASTEST MAN ALIVE

VITAL STATS

LIKES: Speed
DISLIKES: Staying still
FRIENDS: Batman,
Wonder Woman
FOES: The Riddler, Gorilla
Grodd, Captain Cold
SKILLS: Extreme speed
GEAR: Cowl, fast legs

SET NAMES: Batman:
The Riddler Chase, Gorilla
Grodd Goes Bananas
SET NUMBERS: 76012,
76026
YEARS: 2014, 2015

Remove the helmet
to find a two-sided
face complete with a
red mask surround.

Exclusive
helmet with
yellow bolts
on each side

Flip the head to
reveal an angry
expression

Costume printing
continues onto
the back of
the minifigure

Flash insignia

THE NEED FOR SPEED

The Flash was on hand to help
Batman chase down the Riddler's
dragster. With his acrobatic
abilities he jumps over the
Riddler's bombs (and bananas),
and remains in hot pursuit of
the questionable criminal.

DID YOU KNOW?

The Flash appears in
the LEGO *Batman 2: DC
Comics Super Heroes*
and LEGO *Batman 3:
Beyond Gotham*
video games.

After he was struck by lightning,
police scientist Barry Allen developed
the power to run at high speeds. Able
to outrun anything on the planet,
The Flash rushed into a life fighting
crime and was one of the founding
members of the Justice League.

THE RIDDLER
CRIME IN THE FAST LANE

VITAL STATS
....

LIKES: Anything green
DISLIKES: Red lights
FRIENDS: None
FOES: Batman, The Flash
SKILLS: Racing dragsters
GEAR: Question mark
cane, money

SET NAME: Batman:
The Riddler Chase
SET NUMBER: 76012
YEAR: 2014

New bowler hat
with purple
question mark

Purple driving
gloves

Exclusive green
jacket with question
mark motif

BY HOOK OR BY CROOK
When not posing riddles, the
Riddler likes to rob banks and
drive away fast. He is even
armed with a question-mark
shaped crook to stop anyone
who tries to get in his way.

Two-tone
green on legs
and arms

Unquestionably, the Riddler is
one snappy dresser. From his new
racing green hat to his two-tone
legs, the peculiar villain is
committed to his theme: His back
features question marks galore and
the ends of a purple scarf.

THE RIDDLER'S DRAGSTER
QUIZZY AND WHIZZY!

VITAL STATS
....

OWNER: The Riddler
USED FOR: Quick getaways
GEAR: Bomb, moneybags

SET NAME: Batman:
The Riddler Chase
SET NUMBER: 76012
YEAR: 2014

Supercharged engine for extra speed

Flaming gas shoots from the exhaust pipes!

Riddler's question-mark symbol is decorated with flames

CASHBACK!
The back of the Dragster features a spring-loaded mechanism to launch a bomb, plus a pair of moneybags stuffed with cash. These sacks can also be worn on the Riddler's back.

Guess who owns this ultra-fast dragster! The colour and the repeated question mark can only mean the Riddler. He doesn't care who sees him race away from his latest bank robbery, however. He thinks he's far too fast to be caught.

BATMAN OF ZUR-EN-ARRH
THE ALIEN KNIGHT

DID YOU KNOW?
This version of the Caped Crusader first appeared in a 1940 Batman story called *The Superman of Planet X*.

Purple cowl

Two-sided face with stubble and growl on one side and smile on the other

Plain purple cape

EXTRA-SPECIAL EXTRA-TERRESTRIAL
The alien Batman's garish colours continue on the minifigure's back. You can also see his yellow Utility Belt complete with pockets and Tiano's radio, capable of scrambling security systems.

Alien scientist Tiano spent years monitoring Earth. Impressed by Batman, Tiano become a cowled Caped Crusader for his home planet, Zur-En-Arrh. This colourful minifigure was an exclusive Comic-Con release.

ROBIN
READY FOR ACTION

VITAL STATS

LIKES: Staying up late
DISLIKES: School nights
FRIENDS: Batman
FOES: Too many to mention
SKILLS: Acrobatics
GEAR: Grappling hook

SET NAMES: Batman Classic TV Series *Batmobile*, Batman: Defend the Batcave
SET NUMBERS: SDCC037, 10672
YEAR: 2014

Wide open yell

Unique head only available on this minifigure

Shorter yellow cape

Green legs adjoin separate red hip piece

JUNIOR CRIME FIGHTER
Although this Boy Wonder was included as a San Diego Comic-Con exclusive, his true home is in this LEGO® Juniors set. Here he can be found working at his Robin-coloured computer and leaping cheerfully off a building to come to Batman's aid!

Fresh-faced and sporting a look inspired by the 1960s *Batman* TV series, Dick Grayson is back in his classic Robin costume. In a style similar to his original 2006 and 2008 variants, Robin once again wears bright primary colours.

BATMAN
EARLY KNIGHT

VITAL STATS
....

LIKES: Helping young builders
DISLIKES: Complicated instructions
FRIENDS: Robin
FOES: The Joker
SKILLS: Driving
GEAR: Batarang

SET NAMES: Batman Classic TV Series *Batmobile*, Batman: Defend the Batcave
SET NUMBERS: SDCC037, 10672
YEAR: 2014

A new light blue cowl covers Batman's two-sided head

Exclusive bright blue cape only found on this Batman minifigure

Similar body print to the 2012 Batman minifigure

TO THE BATCAVE...

Also starring as a San Diego Comic-Con exclusive, this Batman prefers the home comforts of his LEGO Juniors Batcave in set 10672. However, he needs to fight off the Joker before he can rest easy again...

Available with a LEGO Juniors set, this Batman opts for a friendly bright blue and grey costume. Sticking with a simple theme, he wears a streamlined Utility Belt and a classic yellow bat-symbol.

BATMOBILE
RETRO ROCKET CAR

VITAL STATS
••••••••••••••••••••••••

OWNER: Batman
USED FOR: Crusading capers
GEAR: On-board computer

SET NAME: Batman Classic
TV Series *Batmobile*
SET NUMBER: SDCC037
YEAR: 2014

Two front
windshields

Light warns
other road users
to clear the way

Aerials transmit calls
to the Batphone

RARE RELEASE

This rare set was available only
at the 2014 San Diego Comic-
Con event. It came with Batman
and Robin minifigures, and was
released to mark 75 years of
Batman adventures.

Groovy red trim

DID YOU KNOW?

This set is based on
the Batmobile from
the 1960s *Batman*
TV series.

This unusual-looking Batmobile
has a separate seating compartment
for both Batman and Robin. Powered
by atomic batteries, it has a turbo-
boosting rocket at the rear that
blasts a jet of flame. Lucky there's a
bright red warning light on the top!

ROBIN
THE SON OF BATMAN

Cross expression

Robin's shorter cape looks long on smaller Damian.

Short legs

THE BRAT WONDER

Damian is small but has plenty of attitude. He immediately redesigned the Robin costume and insignia. But, as his alternative face shows, he's often shocked when his father puts him in his place.

Damian is the son of Bruce Wayne. Brought up by his assassin mother, Damian is a skilled, but extremely spoilt, child. On arriving in Gotham City he demanded that he take on the role of Robin. Tim Drake reluctantly stood aside.

BATGIRL
THE COMMISSIONER'S DAUGHTER

VITAL STATS
....

LIKES: Being part of a team
DISLIKES: Being ignored
FRIENDS: Batman, Robin
FOES: The Joker, the
Joker's Goon
SKILLS: Acrobatic tricks
GEAR: Batarang

SET NAME: Batman:
The Joker Steamroller
SET NUMBER: 76013
YEAR: 2014

Double-sided head showing a smile and a frown

Cowl comes complete with red hair

Bright purple cape similar in design to Batman's cape

GIRL POWER

At first Batman wasn't sure about Batgirl. But she soon proved her worth in fights with Gotham City's underworld — from the Joker's henchman to the Clown Prince of Crime himself. In a fight, her trusty Batarang is always by her side!

Torso printing displays a cheerful yellow bat-symbol

Commissioner Gordon's daughter Barbara had always been a Batman fan. She soon follows in the Dark Knight's footsteps, but she has to work hard to keep her identity secret from her detective dad.

THE JOKER'S HENCHMAN
THE GRUMPY GOON

VITAL STATS
....

LIKES: Destruction
DISLIKES: Smiling
FRIENDS: The Joker
FOES: Batman, Robin, Batgirl
SKILLS: Deconstruction
GEAR: Crowbar

SET NAME: Batman:
The Joker Steamroller
SET NUMBER: 76013
YEAR: 2014

Hard hat

Angry face shows
through splotchy
clown make-up

Orange
construction
vest is new and
exclusive for
this variant of
the Joker's goon.

Tool of
destruction

A JOKER ORIGINAL
A quick glance at the
henchman's back shows that the
Joker has been busy customising
his goon's bright orange
wardrobe. The fiend enjoys
a play on words.

The Joker's right-hand goon still
hasn't cheered up. You would think
that the miserable minifigure could
at least manage a smirk. After all,
he has been given free rein by his
boss to demolish Gotham City.
Some people are never happy.

THE JOKER
THE GIGGLING GANGSTER

LEGO fedora rarely seen in this purple hue.

VITAL STATS

LIKES: Looking good
DISLIKES: Being scruffy
FRIENDS: His henchman
FOES: Batman, Robin, Batgirl
SKILLS: Causing devastation
GEAR: Popgun

SET NAME: Batman:
The Joker Steamroller
SET NUMBER: 76013
YEAR: 2014

DID YOU KNOW?
This minifigure's design was inspired by the 1989 *Batman* movie.

Lopsided evil grin

The Joker also wears this lurid torso combination in Jokerland (set 76035).

MONSTER MOTORS
It was no laughing matter when the Joker's Steam Roller carved a crazy path through Gotham City. But Joker's popgun couldn't save him from the combined might of Batman, Robin, and Batgirl.

A criminal mastermind can still take care of his appearance. This outrageous outfit betrays the Joker's gangster roots, adding a little sinister style to the proceedings. And of course, he's still smiling.

THE JOKER'S STEAM ROLLER
DEVASTATINGLY FUNNY

VITAL STATS
....

OWNER: The Joker
USED FOR: Crushing sarcasm
GEAR: Giant roller,
laughing-gas bombs

SET NAMES: Batman: The
Joker Steam Roller
SET NUMBERS: 76013
YEARS: 2014

Toothy
lipstick grin

Laughing-
gas bomb

WHAT A GAS!
The Joker's laughing-
gas bombs are really laughing!
They have wicked grins, evil
eyes, big red clown's noses,
and can be fired from both
sides of the Steam Roller.

Joke gun with
"BANG!" flag

Roller crushes
everything in
its path.

The jokes fall flat when this
wild-looking wagon rolls into view.
It may have a massive grin on the
front, but there's nothing funny
about a demolition drive through
downtown Gotham City.

BATWING
A WING AND A SNARE

VITAL STATS
....
OWNER: Batman
USED FOR: Surprise swoops
GEAR: Missiles, "attack mode" wings

SET NAME: Batman: The Joker Steam Roller
SET NUMBER: 76013
YEAR: 2014

Batman leans back in the streamlined cockpit.

Powerful jet engines

Two missiles on each wing

LEGO Technic elements allow the wings to move.

GRAB AND GO
When it switches to attack mode, the Batwing can bring its two wings together in a pincer movement to snatch unsuspecting villains up from the ground below!

Every bat needs wings, even Batman! This very special Batwing is equipped with four missiles and a surprise attack mode. It's the perfect choice to gain the advantage of height when the Joker takes to the streets with his Steam Roller.

BATMAN
DARK KNIGHT RISING

VITAL STATS
....

LIKES: Armoured vehicles
DISLIKES: Panic in the streets
FRIENDS: Jim Gordon
FOES: The Joker
SKILLS: Driving
GEAR: Batarang

SET NAME: The Tumbler
SET NUMBER: 76023
YEAR: 2014

Exclusive two-sided face not found on another Batman minifigure.

Unique, beefed-up armour

DID YOU KNOW?
This minifigure is based on the costume worn by Batman in the movie *Batman Begins* and the first half of *The Dark Knight*.

Bronze Utility Belt

READY TO TUMBLE
The other side of this minifigure's double-sided head shows a calm, considerate expression. Batman won't remain calm when he takes the Tumbler out on Gotham City's streets.

It's the Darkest Knight of all. After hanging up the cape and cowl, Bruce comes out of retirement as Batman. Gotham City is more dangerous than ever, meaning that his Batsuit is now more body armour than costume.

120

THE JOKER
THE DARK KNIGHT'S DARKEST VILLAIN

DID YOU KNOW?
This minifigure is based on the Joker's appearance in the 2008 *The Dark Knight* movie.

Wide grin flashes yellow teeth

The Joker's face, hair, torso and legs are all exclusive to this one set.

The Joker's torso displays four layers of clothing: a checked shirt, two waistcoats and a purple jacket!

WILD SIDE
The alternative faces on this exclusive minifigure show two equally scary expressions. Added to this, the Joker's wild, scruffy hair is a far cry from his usual styled locks and the dark eye make-up further adds up to a sinister first impression.

Wallet chain

This minifigure of the Joker has a natural skin tone smothered in chalk-white make-up and a painted on smile. But there's nothing funny about his terrible crimes. The Joker has never been so unpredictable. Batman had better watch out!

TUMBLER
ULTIMATE CRIME FIGHTER'S SERIES

Six flaps add drag
for sudden stops

Entry/exit by
top hatch

DID YOU KNOW?
This Ultimate
Collector's Series set
is the largest LEGO DC
Comics Super Heroes
set to date, with
1,869 pieces.

These front tyres
are not found in
any other set

Lights used
when not in
stealth mode

Hydraulic
rods deploy
attack mode

COMPLETE CONTROLS

Two panels lift off the roof
of the Tumbler to reveal an
incredibly detailed cockpit, with
two control panels, several
display screens, steering
controls, and a moving LEGO
gear lever.

This feat of engineering takes
Batman's car collection to a whole
new scale! Its huge tyres provide
traction, while its angular armour
seems to go on forever. At the
back, 1,500 horsepower blasts
out via a giant jet turbine engine.

SUPERBOY
THE BOY OF STEEL

VITAL STATS
....

LIKES: Being a hero
DISLIKES: Being called Superboy
FRIENDS: Superman
FOES: Lex Luthor
SKILLS: Flight, Super-strength
GEAR: Doesn't need any!

SET NAME: Minifigure Gift Set
SET NUMBER: 5004076
YEAR: 2014

DID YOU KNOW?
Superboy's first LEGO appearance was in the videogame LEGO *Batman 2: DC Super Heroes*, where he wore an all-black outfit.

Same tousled hair as Robin (p.13)

Muscle tone shows through tight shirt

Rare two-tone minifigure arms gives t-shirt effect

Blue jeans show Superboy's casual approach to costumes!

A LIKELY LAD
In 2015 exclusive set 5004077 revealed another Super Hero from faraway: Lightning Lad. This character's ability to create eletricity is shown with the dramatic lightning bolts on his minifigure's torso and legs.

Conner Kent was cloned from Lex Luthor and Superman's DNA, but still became Superman's pal, earning the Kryptonian name Kon-El. He has similar abilities to Superman, such as super strength, heat vision, x-ray vision, freeze breath and flight.

GREEN LANTERN
GUARDIAN OF EARTH

VITAL STATS
....

LIKES: Protecting the Earth
DISLIKES: Losing his Lantern
FRIENDS: Batman
FOES: Sinestro
SKILLS: Space flight
GEAR: Green Lantern

SET NAME: Green Lantern vs Sinestro
SET NUMBER: 76025
YEAR: 2015

Green Lantern shares a hairpiece with Commissioner Gordon.

A two-sided head features a grinning face on the reverse

Green Lantern uniform complete with the insignia of the Lantern Corps

DOWN-TO-EARTH
An earlier Green Lantern, based on the 2011 *Green Lantern* movie, was given away to 1,500 raffle winners at the 2011 San Diego Comic-Con, with a smaller quantity released at New York Comic Con the same year.

Black and green printing continues on the back.

When test pilot Hal Jordan discovered the wreckage of an alien spacecraft he received a power ring that transformed him into the Green Lantern. Drawing power from his cosmic lantern, Hal protects the solar system from attack.

SINESTRO
FALLEN LANTERN

VITAL STATS

LIKES: Absolute power
DISLIKES: Hal Jordan
FRIENDS: The Sinestro Corps
FOES: Green Lantern, Batman
SKILLS: Lantern-napping
GEAR: Power staff

SET NAME: Green Lantern vs Sinestro
SET NUMBER: 76025
YEAR: 2015

Double-sided head with a snarling face on the back

Uniquely bright pink face

Symbol of the Sinestro Corps

Yellow and black printing continues on the back of the minifigure.

LANTERN LIFT-OFF
Sinestro stole Hal Jordan's Lantern and placed it within a protective cage on his home planet of Korugar. It has just enough space for one object – either the Lantern or Sinestro himself!

Once considered the greatest Green Lantern of them all, Sinestro was actually using his great powers to enslave alien races. Stripped of his power ring, Sinestro formed the evil Sinestro Corps and became the Green Lantern's sworn enemy.

SPACE BATMAN
COSMIC CAPED CRUSADER

Silver cowl with shorter ears

Wings in closed formation

Air tubes for breathing in space

Space suit printed on both sides of body

SPACE FLIGHT
The Space Batman variant comes with two translucent plastic capes. Remove Batman's rocket pack to switch over to the outstretched bat-wings and take flight after Sinestro.

Silver arms and legs

In space, two heads are better than one. The first is printed with a special visor and breathing apparatus, while this Cosmic Caped Crusader variant also comes with a separate, standard two-sided head.

CONSTRUCT SPACESHIP
IMAGINE THAT!

DID YOU KNOW?
Green Lantern can use his power ring to make solid constructs of anything he imagines – not just spaceships!

Shooters on both wings

Forward shooters

A GIANT LEAP...
The Green Lantern vs Sinestro set also comes with a special Super Jumper piece that serves as a springboard for minifigures to perform giant leaps.

Made from energy channelled through a power ring, this spaceship only works while Green Lantern is concentrating! Hal Jordan creates it to chase after Sinestro, when the villain steals his Power Battery and takes it to the planet Korugar.

WONDER WOMAN
AMAZONIAN WARRIOR

Face printing appears in six other sets

Silver tiara

New battle-ready uniform exclusive to set

SWORD HELD HIGH

A twist of Wonder Woman's head reveals her scowling as she rushes into the fray, armed with her Amazonian sword. She's a foe to be reckoned with thanks to a lifetime of combat training.

Trousers replace her satin tights

Fighting crime in a modern age, the new Wonder Woman is based on an updated costume first introduced to the comics in 2011. Her armour is also printed on the back of her minifigure. Villains beware, this Wonder Woman is ready for battle.

INVISIBLE JET
NOTHING TO SEE HERE!

Hinged cockpit
canopy

Transparent
blue shooter

DID YOU KNOW?
Wonder Woman's
Invisible Jet can also
travel into outer
space – but only for
short periods
of time.

Missile
launcher
without
shooter

GORILLA TACTICS
Wonder Woman uses her
Invisible Jet to come to the
rescue of a Truck Driver (p.133)
in the Gorilla Grodd Goes Bananas
set. The driver probably wishes
he was invisible, too!

Unique transparent
wing pieces

Wonder Woman built the
Invisible Jet in the name of peace.
By travelling unseen, she can carry
out her missions without starting
a fight. The plane is super-fast and
a complete stealth vehicle. Even
the exhaust flames are invisible!

BATMAN
NEW KNIGHT

VITAL STATS

LIKES: New technology
DISLIKES: Low morals
FRIENDS: Wonder Woman,
The Flash
FOES: Gorilla Grodd,
Captain Cold
SKILLS: Piloting his Bat-Mech
GEAR: Batarang

SET NAMES: Gorilla Grodd
Goes Bananas, Batboat
Harbor Pursuit
SET NUMBERS: 76026,
76034
YEAR: 2015

Cape made from new
fabric material

New chinless black
cowl similar to
Batman's space
suit helmet

Body armour
with larger black
bat-symbol

Two-sided head

BOOT-LEGGER BATMAN

The Batman minifigure from
Jokerland (set 76035) is the
only variant to feature a pair
of boots. Complete with a dark
gray suit and golden Utility Belt,
he is ready to take the Gotham
City underworld by storm!

Like Wonder Woman, this Batman
minifigure is based on new costume
designs first introduced to the
comics in 2011. Batman now wears
detailed body armour printed on the
front and back of the minifigure.

CAPTAIN COLD
HOODED HOODLUM

Protective hood

Coolly confident grin

Warm parka printing on both sides of the minifigure

CHILLED TO THE BONE

Captain Cold's alternative face shows his features frozen into a frown. Perhaps facing the Batman wasn't the best idea – after all, the Caped Crusader has plenty of icy experience with Mr Freeze!

When crook Leonard Snart was captured by The Flash, the embarrassed villain swore he'd get revenge. Using his cool intellect Snart created a chilling gun that could freeze anyone in their tracks, including the super-speedy Flash!

GORILLA GRODD
GOING APE

LIKES: Bananas
DISLIKES: Rotten fruit
FRIENDS: Captain Cold
FOES: The Flash, Batman, Wonder Woman
SKILLS: Mind control
GEAR: Banana

SET NAME: Gorilla Grodd Goes Bananas
SET NUMBER: 76026
YEAR: 2015

Mind control equipment

DID YOU KNOW?
Gorilla Grodd made his comic debut in issue 106 of *The Flash* back in 1959.

JUST BANANAS
If there's one thing Gorilla Grodd loves, it's trying to take over the world. But if there's another thing he loves, it's nice tasty bananas. So much so that he attacks this unsuspecting truck driver.

Once Grodd was just another gorilla living in a rainforest. That was until a crashed alien spacecraft gave the great ape hyper-intelligence. Now Grodd is able to telepathically control minds!

TRUCK DRIVER
DRIVEN AROUND THE BEND

VITAL STATS

LIKES: Delivering fruit
DISLIKES: Angry customers, telepathic gorillas
FRIENDS: Batman, the Flash, Wonder Woman
FOES: Gorilla Grodd
SKILLS: Driving
GEAR: Bananas

SET NAME: Gorilla Grodd Goes Bananas
SET NUMBER: 76026
YEAR: 2015

Terrified expression

Back printing shows that this driver works for "Banana Co."

Happy banana logo

Practical dungarees

A BAD DAY AT WORK

First his truck is raided, then he's swung upside-down by a very hungry Grodd! It's shaping up to be a bad day for the truck driver. Frequent super-villain attacks mean there are lots of job vacancies in Gotham City as workers flee from danger.

Talk about being in the wrong place at the wrong time. All the Truck Driver had to do was deliver a batch of bright yellow bananas to Gotham City's fruit lovers. Easy – unless you run into a giant hyper-intelligent gorilla.

BAT-MECH
DESTINED FOR BIG THINGS

Batman at the controls

Arms can move in all directions

Wing armour

Net-shooter arm

Twin stud shooters

NET-WORKING

Batman can catch criminals with one hand using his Bat-Mech! The vehicle's right hand is a cannon containing a net that flies out to ensnare villains at the touch of a button. On this occasion, The Flash came along to help rope up Grodd, too.

Broad feet for balance

A rare LEGO thumb!

Batman designed this Bat-Mech for one-on-one combat with giant-sized bad guys like Gorilla Grodd. Its multi-jointed arms and legs are a match for the most flexible of foes, and its size and strength makes it one of the city's real big-hitters!

SEA SAUCER
FISH DISH

VITAL STATS

OWNER: Black Manta
USED FOR: Underwater villainy
GEAR: Torpedo launchers

SET NAME: Black Manta Deep Sea Strike
SET NUMBER: 76027
YEAR: 2015

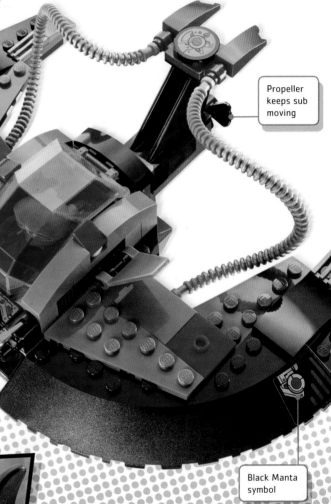

Propeller keeps sub moving

The cockpit even has room for a minifigure with a big helmet!

Torpedo launcher

Black Manta symbol

MEGA BITE

Think sharks are scary? Wait until you see this roboshark! Armed with laser shooters on both sides, the swimming cyborg is controlled by Black Manta from inside his Sea Saucer.

Roguish Black Manta wants to rule the oceans from this stealthy submarine. He uses it to take Robin prisoner in the ruined underwater world of Atlantis, and fires its torpedos at Batman and Aquaman when they launch a rescue attempt.

BLACK MANTA
DEEP-SEA DANGER

VITAL STATS

LIKES: Fishing
DISLIKES: The sea
FRIENDS: None
FOES: Aquaman, Batman
SKILLS: Deep-sea diving
GEAR: Spear, Torpedo-toting robo-shark

SET NAME: Black Manta Deep Sea Strike
SET NUMBER: 76027
YEAR: 2015

There's no minifigure head beneath that oversized helmet.

Tubes take air into the helmet

SUPER SUIT

Although Black Manta has no superpowers, he's a formidable foe. His custom-made scuba suit can survive the extreme pressure of the seabed, fire lasers from his eyes, and shoot electric bolts. He's also armed with a spear for closer attacks.

Scuba suit printing continues on the back

The heavy helmet-wearing Black Manta wants to plunge the ocean's depths for treasure and won't rest until he rules the underwater world for himself. The mysterious villain views Aquaman as his enemy, along with anyone who sides with him.

SCUBA ROBIN
SUBMARINE SIDEKICK

VITAL STATS
....

LIKES: Scuba diving
DISLIKES: Chains
FRIENDS: Batman, Aquaman
FOES: Black Manta
SKILLS: Calling for help
GEAR: Handcuffs

SET NAME: Black Manta
Deep Sea Strike
SET NUMBER: 76027
YEAR: 2015

Under the goggles, this side of Robin's face reveals printed-on scuba gear.

Yellow air-tank attached around neck

DID YOU KNOW?
This minifigure also comes with a black hairpiece for when you remove Robin's helmet.

UNDERWATER PRISON
No wonder a twist of Robin's head reveals a scared expression. Not only does Black Manta slap-on the handcuffs, he also attaches a chain to Robin's legs to anchor him to the seabed.

Flippers attach directly to feet

Robin was enjoying a quick dip beneath the waves when Black Manta clapped him in chains and whisked him away in his sinister Sea Saucer. Robin's crime-fighting career has never sunk so low, but he is at least dressed for the occasion.

BATMAN
BACK UNDERWATER

VITAL STATS

LIKES: Firing torpedoes
DISLIKES: Soggy sidekicks
FRIENDS: Robin, Aquaman
FOES: Black Manta
SKILLS: Piloting the Bat Sub
GEAR: Batarang

SET NAME: Black Manta Deep Sea Strike
SET NUMBER: 76027
YEAR: 2015

Uses a similar double-sided head to the previous Scuba minifigure

A newer softer cape

TEST DIVE
Even though Black Manta abducting the Boy Wonder is annoying, it does give Batman a chance to test the brand new Bat Sub. Not all bad, then!

With the same body as the Jokerland Batman, this deep-sea Detective also uses a revised cowl. The new helmet doesn't include a chin guard, so there's printing of the mask on Batman's head itself.

BAT SUB
DOUBLE DIVER

Rudder turns to steer sub

DID YOU KNOW?
Scuba stands for "self-contained underwater breathing apparatus".

Mini sub docks here

VITAL STATS

OWNER: Batman
USED FOR: Deep-sea missions
GEAR: Mini sub, torpedoes

SET NAME: Black Manta Deep Sea Strike
SET NUMBER: 76027
YEAR: 2015

Torpedo launcher

Wheel to open engine compartment

SECONDARY SUB
Dressed in his scuba gear, Robin powers through the water by holding onto the back of this mini sub. When not in use, it connects to the main Bat Sub.

Engine heat vent

More like a shark than a bat, this long, slim sub slices through water at high speed, in search of its prey: the villainous Black Manta! It is actually two underwater vehicles in one, with a small, detachable glider docked at the back.

GREEN ARROW
ANGRY ARCHER

Face stubble printing reveals that the Green Archer is in need of a shave.

Green plastic hood hangs from around the neck.

ARMED AND DANGEROUS
You can swivel the Green Arrow's head to reveal an angry expression. A quiver full of arrows is also printed on the back of his torso, beneath his cape.

Standard LEGO bow and arrow in green.

With a body similar to the earlier San Diego Comic-Con exclusive, this Green Arrow has plain green legs rather than kneepads. Luckily for the Justice League, the Arrow stays on target no matter what his workday wardrobe.

THE JAVELIN
THE JUSTIC LEAGUE'S SPACESHIP

Double doors open to reveal large cargo bay

DID YOU KNOW?
Darkseid Invasion was the first set to include a springy Super Jumper element – hidden in the Javelin's cargo bay.

Justice League emblem on nose cone

A lever can tilt the wing tips upwards for landing.

JAW-DROPPING
The underside of the Javelin has two rocket launchers and a bomb door that opens like a jaw to drop its cargo – or to scoop up an enemy minifigure!

There is room inside the cockpit for Green Arrow's bow alongside the archer.

Green Arrow flies this sleek Justice League jet, which can travel through air, underwater or in the vacuum of space. It was built by Batman and is equipped with all the gadgets and gear you'd expect from him – just not in his usual dark colour scheme!

DARKSEID
OVERSIZED ALIEN OVERLORD

Cracked grey
skin

Darkseid's red eyes can
launch laser beams.

Huge gripping hand

CANNONBALL CHAOS
Darkseid's invasion starts
in Metropolis, when the alien
overlord plays skittles with
skyscrapers, blasting cannonballs
from a Hover Launcher enlarged
for his oversized form.

The tyrannical ruler of Apokolips
has set his eyes on the rest of the
universe. Invulnerable to anything
but his own eye-beams, Darkseid
is super-strong and resourceful.
Nothing will stop his takeover plans.

HAWKMAN
WINGED WARRIOR

Golden helmet also winged to be aerodynamic.

Wings attach to Hawkman's minifigure using gold studs.

BEATING WINGS
Hawkman comes with two interchangeable set of plastic wings, one spread out for flight and the other drawn in for fight! There's also a two-sided head beneath that helmet.

Hawk symbol joins crossing chest straps.

Archaeologist Carter Hall uses magical Nth Metal to soar through the air as the savage Hawkman. This Justice League member is no young featherweight – he's actually a reincarnated Egyptian prince!

CYBORG
MECHANICAL WHIZZ

Stud Shooter keeps
villains at bay.

Snarling face partially
covered by Cyborg's
cybernetic helmet.

METALLIC MAGNETISM
In the Justice League, Cyborg
uses his varied skills to fend off
many villains, including Brainiac.
In LEGO *Batman 2: DC Super
Heroes* Cyborg temporarily has
useful magnetic powers!

Leg printing
reveals extensive
metallic parts.

When Vic Stone was injured, his
father rebuilt him as half-man, half-
machine. Becoming Cyborg, he can
interface with computers, although
rumors that he uses his advanced
cybernetics to cheat while playing
Batman at video games aren't true!

HOVER DESTROYER
DARKSEID'S HOVERBOARD

VITAL STATS

OWNER: Darkseid
USED FOR: Fighting flying
Super Heroes
GEAR: Omega cannon

SET NAMES: Darkseid
Invasion
SET NUMBERS:
76028
YEARS: 2015

Large levers
for Darkseid's
huge hands

Bright red balls
of Omega energy
are launched from
this cannon.

Space to store
second cannonball
behind launcher

Omega symbol on
front of craft

BALANCING ACT

Darkseid positions his brawny
bulk at the back of the Hover
Destroyer, standing on special
footholds. From this secure
stance he takes on a full cohort
of Superman, Green Arrow,
Cyborg, and Hawkman.

Darkseid can match Superman
with many alien powers, but one
thing that he can't do is fly! It
takes three anti-gravity discs to
lift the muscular monster on this
floating weapons platform, along
with his heavy, high-tech cannon.

SUPERMAN
FLYING TO THE RESCUE

VITAL STATS
....

LIKES: Working with his cousin
DISLIKES: Alien invasions
FRIENDS: Supergirl,
Martian Manhunter
FOES: Brainiac
SKILLS: Leaping tall buildings
in a single bound
GEAR: Cape

SET NAME: Brainiac Attack
SET NUMBER: 76040
YEAR: 2015

DID YOU KNOW?
The minifigure from
Superman vs Power
Armour Lex also dons
the new cape for the
2015 San Diego
Comic-Con set.

Red eyes
ready to blast
heat vision

SUPER-SWITCHEROO
There's more mix-and-match Man
of Steel with Darkseid Invasion
(set 76028) as the Superman
in this set includes a body and
head from Superman vs Power
Armour Lex (set 6862) plus the
new cape. Phew!

This mixed-up minifigure's body
was originally found in Superman
vs Power Armour Lex (set 6862),
while his head comes from the
Man of Steel movie set. The cape
is brand new however, made from
a new softer, stretchier material.

SUPERGIRL
CAPED COUSIN

DID YOU KNOW?
Supergirl made her first appearance in a 1959 issue of *Action Comics*.

Long flowing blond hair

CROSS KRYPTONIAN
Don't be fooled by Supergirl's calm face – the other side reveals an angry expression and heat-vision eyes. Supergirl shares Superman's power, but she doesn't share his self-restraint and mild-mannered nature!

Supergirl's torso has been adjusted especially for her, and is exclusive to this variant.

What do you get when you cross superpowers with teenage attitude? Plenty of trouble, that's what! Sent to Earth to care for her cousin Kal-El, Kara Zor-El's spacecraft was knocked off course. She actually arrives years after Superman had grown up!

149

THE MARTIAN MANHUNTER
SHAPE-SHIFTING ALIEN

Single-sided green head

Exclusive blue collar for this shape-shifter from Mars

Body printing on front and back based on the Martian Manhunter's classic costume.

ALTERNATIVE ALIEN

An earlier version of the Martian Manhunter minifigure was given away on LEGO.com in March 2014. This one had a costume based on the 2011 comic books, plus a simplified blue cape.

The last survivor of a Martian race, J'onn J'onzz came to Earth to join the Justice League. Able to recover from just about any injury, the Martian Manhunter can take on any form he chooses to solve crimes. He is also a mindreader!

BRAINIAC
LIVING COMPUTER

VITAL STATS
....

LIKES: Knowledge
DISLIKES: Kryptonite
FRIENDS: Gorilla Grodd
FOES: Superman, Supergirl, Martian Manhunter
SKILLS: Genius-level intellect
GEAR: Skull Ship

SET NAME: Brainiac Attack
SET NUMBER: 76040
YEAR: 2015

Purple wiring printed on both sides of minifigure

Computer connections

Lime green hands

DID YOU KNOW?
Brainiac even turned Supergirl's dad into a cyborg, for the crime of being a native of Kandor City.

KANDOR CAPER
Brainiac has clashed with Superman on numerous occasions, ever since the Man of Steel discovered that the alien android had shrunk the Kryptonian city of Kandor.

An alien supercomputer from the planet Colu, Brainiac believes that knowledge is power. In order to understand other races he steals entire cities, shrinking them to fit into jars – usually without asking the inhabitants first.

SKULL SHIP
A HEAD FOR HEIGHTS

VITAL STATS
....

OWNER: Brainiac
USED FOR: Invading Earth
GEAR: Cannons, tentacles

SET NAME: Brainiac Attack
SET NUMBER: 76040
YEAR: 2015

Hyperspace engines

Scary skull face

Laser cannon docks here

Terrifying tentacles!

Twin laser cannons

DOME ALONE

The transparent green dome of Brainiac's Skull Ship is not found in any other LEGO set, though a trans-clear version is used in two LEGO® Space Alien Conquest sets from 2011: UFO Abduction (set 7052) and Alien Mothership (set 7065).

Alien Super Villain Brainiac controls his scary Skull Ship with the power of his mind. He can cause chaos with its two laser cannons and six twisty tentacles, and gets a 360-degree view of the action from its grisly green protective dome.

BATZARRO
THE WORLD'S WORST DETECTIVE

VITAL STATS
....

LIKES: Committing crimes
DISLIKES: Batman
FRIENDS: Bizarro
FOES: The Justice League
SKILLS: Causing chaos
GEAR: Tattered Cape

SET NAME: LEGO DC Comics Super Heroes: Justice League vs Bizarro League DVD/Blu-Ray
SET NUMBER: N/A
YEAR: 2015

DID YOU KNOW?
One of Batzarro's ambitions is to meet his number one hero—the Joker!

Double-sided head showing Batzarro snarling

Upside down bat-symbol and Utility Belt

Cape in tatters

SWITCHING SIDES
Batzarro is growling on one side of his head. He may look scary, but in the end he teams up with the real Batman and the Justice League to defeat Darkseid.

Created by Bizarro using his LexCorp duplicator ray, Batzarro is a weird mixed-up version of the Dark Knight Detective and a member of the Bizarro League. While Batman is super-smart, Batzarro is, well, not.

153

DEATHSTROKE
MERCENARY THIEF

VITAL STATS

LIKES: Diamonds
DISLIKES: Being chased
FRIENDS: None
FOES: Batman, Robin
SKILLS: Piloting his jetboat
GEAR: Sword, gun

SET NAME: Batboat
Harbor Pursuit
SET NUMBER: 76034
YEAR: 2015

Two-colour orange
and black mask

Spare ammo ready
for any mission

Two-tone legs

MASKED MAN

The reverse of Deathstroke's mask features his trademark long headband that the mercenary sometimes wears in the comic books. His bandolier can be seen wrapping around the back of the minifigure.

Before turning to crime, Slade Wilson was a marine who was transformed into a soldier by the U.S. military. Tackling weapon-expert Deathstroke is always dangerous, especially when he's on the run from his latest diamond heist.

ROBIN
TEENAGE WONDER

DID YOU KNOW?
This minifigure reuses the Robin headpiece from Batman: The Joker Steam Roller (set 76013).

Longer hair

New hi-tech body armour

RADAR ROBIN
There was nowhere to hide for Deathstroke as Batman and Robin took to the Batboat. Robin used the Bat-radar to track down the menacing mercenary.

Dick Grayson may be moving on to fight crime as Nightwing, but he still reappears as Robin every now and again. He can't wait for Batman to let him pilot the Batboat for himself and wears this darker suit in a fight against Deathstroke.

BATBOAT
BATMAN'S CATAMARAN

DID YOU KNOW?
A catamaran is a boat with two hulls – not to be confused with a Batarang!

Radar tower lies flat at high speeds

Empty missile launcher

Levers release hovercraft from main section

VITAL STATS
....
OWNER: Batman
USED FOR: Aquatic adventures
GEAR: Missiles, blasters, radar tower

SET NAME: The Batboat Harbor Pursuit
SET NUMBER: 76034
YEAR: 2015

TOWER OF POWER
The tall radar tower lifts up to reveal a bank of high-tech control screens where Robin can track enemy vessels. But beware – there's a trapdoor hidden underneath!

Each cockpit has its own controls

Front blasters detach with cockpits

Batman and Robin are full-steam ahead in this double-hulled Batboat! Its cockpits can split off to become two hovercraft armed with blasters. The remaining control center runs on autopilot with a retractable radar tower defended by missiles.

BATMOBILE
HEROIC HOT ROD

VITAL STATS

OWNER: Batman
USED FOR: Rescue missions
GEAR: Front and back missiles

SET NAME: Jokerland
SET NUMBER: 76035
YEAR: 2015

Jet turbine

Rear weaponry

Detachable cockpit canopy

Turbocharger

DOUBLE DEFENSE
The Batmobile is armed from end to end, with two spring-loaded missiles hidden in the front turbine, and two stud shooters beneath the wings at the back.

This Batmobile is one huge jet engine, with a big round turbine drawing in air at the front, and a turbocharger adding extra power at the back. The roof lifts right off so Batman can leap into action at top speed, too!

STARFIRE
ALIEN PRINCESS

VITAL STATS
....

LIKES: Fun
DISLIKES: Misery
FRIENDS: Robin, Beast
Boy, Batman
FOES: Poison Ivy, Harley
Quinn, the Joker, the Penguin
SKILLS: Flight
GEAR: Starbolt energy,
handcuffs, lock

SET NAME: Jokerland
SET NUMBER: 76035
YEAR: 2015

Double-sided head
shows an anxious
expression

Long flowing
purple hair

Starbolt
energy blasts
made from
green LEGO
plate pieces

STAR BRIGHT
When the Joker took over the
Gotham City Funfair, Starfire
and the Teen Titans flew to
Batman's aid. Plants usually like
light, but Poison Ivy wasn't so
keen on Starfire's starbolts!

The daughter of the Tamaran
king and queen, Princess Koriand'r
absorbs solar energy through her
skin and converts it to the power she
needs to fly and blast emerald energy
bolts from her hands. Now, she fights
alongside Robin in the Teen Titans.

BEAST BOY
THE WILDEST KID ON THE PLANET

VITAL STATS
....

LIKES: Playing tricks
DISLIKES: Being locked up
FRIENDS: Robin,
Starfire, Batman
FOES: The Penguin, the Joker,
Harley Quinn, Poison Ivy
SKILLS: Shape-shifting
GEAR: Staff, handcuffs, lock

SET NAME: Jokerland
SET NUMBER: 76035
YEAR: 2015

Grinning face

Beast Boy's pointed ears are molded to his hairpiece.

Distinctive purple outfit

BEAST VS. BIRD

A real prankster, Beast Boy loves to play practical jokes on his teammates. However, as his alternative face shows, he wasn't so happy to find himself tricked and trapped in a duck prison by the Penguin.

Dark green hands

Garfield Logan is a bit of every animal. The Teen Titan can transform himself into any bird or beast, thanks to a special serum that saved him from a toxic animal bite as a child. Unfortunately it left him with green coloured skin in return!

HARLEY QUINN
HUMOROUS HIGH ROLLER

LIKES: Silly stunts
DISLIKES: Being serious
FRIENDS: The Joker, Poison Ivy, the Penguin
FOES: Robin, Batman, Starfire, Beast Boy
SKILLS: Stunt riding
GEAR: Giant hammer, stunt motorcycle

SET NAME: Jokerland
SET NUMBER: 76035
YEAR: 2015

This is the first Harley minifigure not to feature her eye mask.

New body printing complete with bells around Harley's neck

DID YOU KNOW?
This outfit was based on a new costume first introduced to the comics in 2014.

HIGH-WIRE HAVOC
Harley's "Wheels of Fire" motorcycle can be sent rolling down its slope with a flick of a sign. Harley is enjoying the ride a lot more than the upside-down Robin stuck underneath!

Printing continues on the side of Harley's legs

Red and black gloves

In her new acrobat suit, the Clown Princess of Crime doesn't wear her usual mask, opting for dark make-up around her eyes. She still loves a laugh though, and uses her over-sized weapon to hammer home any punch line.

ROBIN
TEEN TITAN

VITAL STATS
....

LIKES: Leading his team
DISLIKES: Getting caught
FRIENDS: Starfire, Beast Boy, Batman
FOES: Harley Quinn, the Joker, the Penguin, Poison Ivy
SKILLS: Circus tricks, balance
GEAR: Staff, handcuffs, lock

SET NAME: Jokerland
SET NUMBER: 76035
YEAR: 2015

Spiky hair

Double-sided head showing shocked expression

New stretchy cape

THE FIRST ROBIN

Based on his Teen Titans costume, this minifigure shows Robin with his original insignia and short sleeved arms. A turn of his head shows a determined expression too.

Dick Grayson helped found the Teen Titans, and was certainly pleased to see his teammates when he found himself locked up by Harley Quinn in the Joker's twisted fun-scare. Of course, he claimed getting caught was all part of the plan!

ARSENAL
THE RED ARROW

VITAL STATS
....

LIKES: Fighting crime
DISLIKES: Being called Speedy
FRIENDS: Green Arrow
FOES: Deathstroke
SKILLS: Archery
GEAR: Longbow

SET NAME: Arsenal San Diego Comic-Con Exclusive
SET NUMBER: SDCC2015
YEARS: 2015

Red hood based on the costume from the Arrow TV show

Black version of Green Arrow's longbow

Leather straps printed on chest

READY TO FIRE

The back of the exclusive minifigure shows a quiver of arrows ready to fire. Arsenal also has a double-sided head complete with a snarling face on the reverse.

When Arrow took martial art expert Roy Harper under his wing he tried to call his new sidekick Speedy. Harper hated the name, christening himself Arsenal instead. The young archer is almost as good a shot as his green-hooded mentor.

TRICKSTER
PRANKS A LOT!

VITAL STATS

LIKES: Tricking people
DISLIKES: Being tricked
FRIENDS: Captain Cold
FOES: The Flash
SKILLS: Telling jokes
GEAR: Anti-gravity boots

SET NAMES: LEGO *DC Comics Super Heroes Justice League: Attack of the Legion of Doom!* DVD movie
YEARS: 2015

Two-colour arms suggest T-shirt sleeves

No other LEGO minifigure has hair this colour

Belt and braces lined with gadget pouches

REAR-AXEL

The Trickster's belt and braces printing continues on his back, adding more pouches in which he can store twisted trick items such as itching powder and exploding rubber chickens!

Checkered pattern continues on side of legs

Axel Walker is no ordinary teenage villain. As the Trickster, he uses practical jokes and wacky gadgets to commit his crimes, and has invented a pair of anti-gravity boots that let him run through the air to escape The Flash.

DEADSHOT
MASKED MARKSMAN

VITAL STATS
· ·

LIKES: Moving targets
DISLIKES: Feeling aimless
FRIENDS: Harley Quinn
FOES: Batman
SKILLS: Expert aim
GEAR: Built-in guns and targeting tech

SET NAMES: Batman: Gotham City Cycle Chase
SET NUMBERS: 76053
YEARS: 2016

Gun sight built into mask

Armoured suit can withstand explosions

Wrist-mounted guns on arm

GUN FOR HIGH-UP HIRE
Deadshot is really skyrocketing with this jetpack and bazooka combo! The giant weapon is made from eight pieces and can fire studs on Batman and his friends below.

This sharpshooter likes to boast that he never misses a target. He wears a metal mask with a special eyepiece to help him take aim, and has weapons built in to the arms of his suit. Sometimes he fights crime, but he prefers to battle Batman!

HARLEY QUINN
TRICOLOUR TRICKSTER

VITAL STATS

LIKES: Hair dye
DISLIKES: Being serious
FRIENDS: Deadshot
FOES: Batman
SKILLS: Gymnastics
GEAR: Giant hammer

SET NAMES: Batman: Gotham City Cycle Chase
SET NUMBERS: 76053
YEARS: 2016

Unique red and blue hairpiece

Harley's bare arms are as white as her face!

Brutal belt of bullets

Corset design continues on back

HARLEY GRIM

Harley's double-sided head turns to reveal an angry glare and gritted teeth. It's the face that the chaos-loving criminal wears when she brings out her big hammer!

Harley looks a little blue in her latest outfit, but her evil grin suggests that she's still happy being bad. Her usual jester's hat has been replaced by a pair of mismatched pigtails and her belt is bulked out with a row of bullets!

HARLEY QUINN'S BIKE
DRIVETIME HITS

VITAL STATS
....

OWNER: Harley Quinn
USED FOR: Going flat out
GEAR: Hammer attachment

SET NAMES: Batman:
Gotham City Cycle Chase
SET NUMBERS: 76053
YEARS: 2016

Hammer has
"POW!" written
on one end.

One of four exhausts
needed to power
enormous engine

Bigger wheel
at front

Laser cannons flank
front wheel

WHACK ATTACK
Harley's hammer can be fixed on
to the bike in two different
ways, so that it can swing from
side to side, or back and forth.
It has a diamond design that is
similar to a harlequin's suit.

Harley likes to smash speed
records on her motorcycle. In fact,
she likes to smash everything! Her
massive mallet fits on to the side
of the bike and is ready to whack
anyone overtaking in the next lane.
Batman had better watch out!

BATCYCLE
LONGER, WIDER, STRONGER

VITAL STATS

OWNER: Batman
USED FOR: Narrow escapes
GEAR: Grapple, shooters

SET NAMES: Batman: Gotham City Cycle Chase
SET NUMBERS: 76053
YEARS: 2016

Afterburner glows with heat

Silver Batarang stored at the back

Bat-symbol on fuel tank

ARMED ARMS

Backward-facing shooters on both sides of the rear wheel can flip round and fire to the front or sides. The right-hand arm also has a grapple gun, and the left holds a Batarang.

Laser cannons in front lights

Batman's motorcycle has wheels as wide as he is! The Caped Crusader keeps a low profile between the monster-truck tyres and dual shooters can target enemies tearing away in front of the bike or giving chase behind it.

169

LEX LUTHOR
LEXCORP LEADER

VITAL STATS

LIKES: Having hair, helicopters
DISLIKES: Super Hero team-ups
FRIENDS: Henchmen
FOES: Superman, Wonder Woman, Batman
SKILLS: Computer coding
GEAR: Double-barreled handgun

SET NAMES: Heroes of Justice: Sky-High Battle
SET NUMBERS: 76046
YEARS: 2016

Smart-casual sand-coloured clothes of a tech company boss.

HAIR RAISER

This LexCorp helicopter has eight Kryptonite missiles to launch against Superman – but Lex can't stop Wonder Woman coming to rescue Lois.

Lex luxuriates in long hair and a leisure suit for his latest, laid-back look. There's nothing relaxed about his grimace and gun however, which he uses to menace Lois Lane. Perhaps he knows he's still bald under that LEGO hair piece!

LEXCORP HENCHMAN
GRIZZLED GUARD

VITAL STATS

LIKES: LexCorp staff benefits
DISLIKES: Not getting to drive the forklift truck
FRIENDS: Other henchmen
FOES: Batman, Superman
SKILLS: Guarding things
GEAR: Bazooka

SET NAMES: Kryptonite Interception
SET NUMBERS: 76045
YEARS: 2016

LexCorp ID badge

Black gloves for doing dirty work

Stud-shooting bazooka rifle

BADDIE BUDDY
The henchman's pal wears the same uniform and a similar scowl, but is clean-shaven. Together they guard a secret stash of LexCorp Kryptonite.

A henchman needs an impressive resumé to work at LexCorp, and this bearded baddie lists guard duty and bazooka skills among his many talents. In return for loyalty to Lex, he gets a smart green uniform and access to high-tech weapons.

ARMOURED BATMAN
GLOWERS IN THE DARK

Glow-in-the-
dark eyes

Chunky
armour
covers
torso

Silver Batarang
fixes on back

BAZOOKA BUILD

Batman's three-in-one weapon
can be built as a stud-shooting
bazooka with two handles, or as
a smaller stud-shooter and a
separate grapple launcher for
Batman to hold in each hand.

Sometimes, even Super Heroes
squabble – and when Batman takes
on Superman in a rooftop duel, he'll
need his most impressive armour!
This combat suit has grips to store
equipment and protective plating.

SUPERMAN
SUITED AND REBOOTED

VITAL STATS
....

LIKES: Saving the world
DISLIKES: Kryptonite missiles
FRIENDS: Lois Lane
FOES: Lex Luthor
SKILLS: Heat vision, X-ray vision
GEAR: Heat vision

SET NAMES: Heroes of Justice: Sky-High Battle
SET NUMBERS: 76046
YEARS: 2016

All versions of Superman have a chiselled jaw, but only this one wears this broad grin.

New LEGO hair piece

Red cape is the only element shared with other Superman minifigures.

Red boots printed on legs

RED-EYE

Superman sports angry red eyes in Clash of the Heroes (set 76044). Maybe it's his heat vision, or perhaps he's cross that he's lost his bright red boots!

Batman and Superman must save Lois from the clutches of Lex Luthor in his LexCorp helicopter. Superman has a whole new outfit with bright red boots, a heroic new hairstyle and alternative expressions on his double-sided face.

173

BATWING
FLYING ALL THROUGH THE NIGHT

VITAL STATS
....

OWNER: Batman
USED FOR: Chasing Lex Luthor
GEAR: Rapid-fire shooter

SET NAMES: Heroes of Justice: Sky-High Battle
SET NUMBERS: 76046
YEARS: 2016

Cockpit opens in two sections

DID YOU KNOW?
The Batwing's rotating cannon has six rapid-fire launchers. Lex Luthor, in his helicopter, needs to watch out!

Small silver bat-symbol on cannon

WINGING IT
In flight, the Batwing gains lift by extending its wings in a "V" formation. In landing mode, its wings retract and its fins fold up to create a smaller and squarer silhouette.

Wings fully extended for flight mode

When Superman is on the scene, Batman needs wings to keep up with the action! The Caped Crusader jumps into this stealth flyer to join the Last Son of Krypton in pursuit of Lex Luthor.

WONDER WOMAN
FIGHTING FOR JUSTICE

VITAL STATS

LIKES: Animals
DISLIKES: War
FRIENDS: Superman
FOES: Lex Luthor
SKILLS: Amazonian martial arts
GEAR: Sword and shield

SET NAMES: Heroes of Justice: Sky-High Battle
SET NUMBERS: 76046
YEARS: 2016

Hair piece is new for 2016.

DID YOU KNOW?
All earlier minifigure versions of Wonder Woman have her royal headband moulded as part of the hair piece.

Gold chestplate is shaped like an eagle.

Bulletproof bracelets on both arms

FACE TO FACE
Wonder Woman's head turns to reveal determined eyes and gritted teeth as she heads into battle. She is armed with her trusty sword and a shield with an eagle motif.

Wonder Woman uses lightning-fast reflexes to deflect bullets with her armour bracelets, and is ready for whatever Lex Luthor can throw at her. She knows that their battle will mean the difference between war and the dawn of justice!

LOIS LANE
STAR OF THE PLANET

VITAL STATS
. . . .

LIKES: Exclusives
DISLIKES: Cover-ups
FRIENDS: Superman
FOES: Lex Luthor
SKILLS: Getting to the truth
GEAR: Camera

SET NAMES: Heroes of
Justice: Sky-High Battle
SET NUMBERS: 76046
YEARS: 2016

Serious face
can be swapped
for scared look

Camera for capturing
breaking news

Smart suit for
doing interviews

A NOSE FOR NEWS

Lois loves to investigate and
often gets into danger following
her reporter's instincts. When
she starts to ask questions
about Lex Luthor, she ends up
hanging from his helicopter!

Ace news reporter Lois Lane
knows Superman's secret, but he
trusts her not to print it in the *Daily
Planet*! With a camera in her hand
and a big story in her sights, there's
nowhere Lois won't go to find the
facts for tomorrow's headlines.

BATMOBILE
CARRIAGE OF JUSTICE

VITAL STATS
....

OWNER: Batman
USED FOR: Getting around
Gotham City
GEAR: Front and side
cannons

SET NAMES: Kryptonite
Interception
SET NUMBERS: 76045
YEARS: 2016

Cockpit
opens in two
sections

Armoured
plates protect
rear wheels

Stud shooters
at front

Recessed
front lights

FORK IN THE ROAD

A forklift truck might seem
like no match for the Batmobile,
but this LexCorp model is armed
with flick missiles and driven
by a henchman with a stud-
shooting bazooka!

Ideal for a trip to Metropolis,
this Batmobile is heavily armed and
armoured against superpowered
attack. Silver details include side
vents and a shield–like bat-symbol
on the hood, plus shiny shooters to
bring a touch of bling to any battle!

BATMAN
BACK WITH A "BAM!"

VITAL STATS
....

LIKES: Law-abiding citizens
DISLIKES: Dastardly traps
FRIENDS: Robin, Alfred
FOES: Catwoman, the Joker,
the Penguin, the Riddler
SKILLS: Science, maths,
grammar
GEAR: Batarang

SET NAMES: *Batman* Classic
TV Series – Batcave
SET NUMBERS: 76052
YEARS: 2016

Cowl with
printed frown

Physique shows
through tight
suit

TRUE OR FALSE?
Batman has all sorts of high-
tech equipment in his Batcave
laboratory, including a huge
atomic reactor, radar screens
and a lie detector with green
and red lights on top.

Trusty
Batarang

Batman is a brilliant inventor and
his unique Utility Belt is full of
gadgets for every occasion. He has
even invented a dance called the
"Batusi". It helps him keep in shape
for his never-ending battle against
the rogues of Gotham City!

BRUCE WAYNE
THE MAN BEHIND THE MASK

Neat, no-nonsense hair

Stylish cravat in open shirt

DID YOU KNOW?
The classic *Batman* TV series ran for three seasons between 1966 and 1968, with a total of 120 episodes.

Wayne family crest on blazer

RED ALERT
As well as being filled with all his sporting trophies, Bruce's study is also home to a bright red telephone. This gives the Gotham City police a direct line to Batman and Robin.

The billionaire owner of Wayne Manor is accomplished at horse riding, fishing, climbing and marbles. He gives money to charity and cares for his young ward, Dick Grayson. On top of that, he has a new sharp suit – and he's also Batman!

ALFRED
FAITHFUL FRIEND

VITAL STATS

LIKES: Dusting and polishing
DISLIKES: Home invasions
FRIENDS: Bruce Wayne,
Dick Grayson
FOES: The Joker
SKILLS: Excellent telephone
manner
GEAR: None

SET NAMES: *Batman* Classic
TV Series – Batcave
SET NUMBERS: 76052
YEARS: 2016

White handkerchief
in breast pocket

Batphone for receiving calls
from Commissioner Gordon

YOU RANG, SIR?
Alfred's daily duties include
answering the Batphone. He
summons Batman if he is at
home, and takes messages from
Commissioner Gordon if the
Caped Crusader is out.

BRUCE

The stately butler of Wayne
Manor, Alfred does much more than
just answer the Batphone. He is a
mechanic, a swordsman and an
archer, and has years of wisdom to
offer the Dynamic Duo. Batman and
Robin would be lost without him!

DICK GRAYSON
WARD OF WAYNE MANOR

VITAL STATS
....

LIKES: Secretly being Robin
DISLIKES: Writing essays
FRIENDS: Bruce Wayne,
Alfred
FOES: Catwoman
SKILLS: Tuba playing,
bird calls
GEAR: None

SET NAMES: *Batman* Classic
TV Series – Batcave
SET NUMBERS: 76052
YEARS: 2016

Dick models his
neat hair after
Bruce Wayne's

Sensible red
jumper over
white shirt

Smart blue
trousers

BATCAVE OR BUST
When duty calls, Dick flips up
the bust of Shakespeare on
Bruce's desk to reveal a hidden
button. Pressing it opens up a
secret entrance to the Batcave!

Being Dick Grayson sure is tough!
His legal guardian, Bruce Wayne,
makes him study hard when he'd
rather be working out in the gym.
But when Bruce explains it's all part
of being a Boy Wonder, Dick
reckons life is not so bad after all.

THE JOKER
CACKLING PRINCE OF CRIME

Greasepaint
covers
moustache

Three-piece
suit packed
with pranks

Beaker full of
potent chemicals

LAB GRAB
When the Joker gets his hands
on Batman's lab, who knows
what chemical concoctions he
will cook up! Going by the grin
on his alternative face, it might
be a batch of laughing gas.

With his grotesque grin, green
hair and bright pink suit, the Joker
is never going to make it as a
sneak thief! Instead he likes to live
large as he launches plots to steal
paintings, build a flying saucer and
beat Batman at a surfing contest.

CATWOMAN
PURRING PLUNDERER

VITAL STATS
....

LIKES: Long stretches
DISLIKES: Long stretches in jail
FRIENDS: The Joker, the
Penguin, the Riddler
FOES: Batman and Robin
SKILLS: Cat burglary
GEAR: Gas-filled whip

SET NAMES: *Batman* Classic
TV Series – Batcave
SET NUMBERS: 76052
YEARS: 2016

Cat ears attached
to hairband

Catty look can
be swapped for
a merrier,
masked face

Gold medallion
worn over catsuit

THE CAT CAME BACK
Catwoman knows all about
Wayne Manor after posing as
Dick Grayson's dance teacher.
She's not scared of falling as
she scales its walls, because a
cat will always land on its feet!

Catwoman would like Batman if
it wasn't for all his do-gooding!
Instead she sets her cat's eyes on
ridding Gotham City of its Dynamic
Duo, and risking her nine lives on
feline felonies such as sneaking
into Wayne Manor!

183

THE RIDDLER
AN ENIGMA

VITAL STATS
....

LIKES: Quizzes and conundrums
DISLIKES: Easy answers
FRIENDS: Catwoman, the Joker, the Penguin
FOES: Batman and Robin
SKILLS: Chemistry, cryptography
GEAR: Dynamite

SET NAMES: *Batman* Classic TV Series – Batcave
SET NUMBERS: 76052
YEARS: 2016

Head rotates to reveal gleeful grin

Dynamite to destroy the Batcave!

RIDDLE ME THIS...
What three letters make the sound of an explosion? TNT! The Riddler is out to blow the roof off Wayne Manor.

Silk cummerbund matches gloves and mask

When does a question mark mean danger? When it's printed on the Riddler's outfit! This puzzling pest always leaves clues to his quizzical crimes, luring Batman and Robin into baffling booby traps that seem to have no answer.

ROBIN
BRIGHT AND BREEZY

VITAL STATS
....

LIKES: Riding in the Batmobile
DISLIKES: Not getting to drive the Batmobile
FRIENDS: Batman, Alfred
FOES: Catwoman, the Joker, the Penguin, the Riddler
SKILLS: Honesty, courage
GEAR: Handcuffs

SET NAMES: *Batman* Classic TV Series – Batcave
SET NUMBERS: 76052
YEARS: 2016

Reverse of head shows alarmed face

Tunic laces up at front

Flesh-coloured tights protect legs

TO THE BATPOLES!
Quick-change Batpoles in the Batcave allow Bruce Wayne and Dick Grayson to become Batman and Robin at the flick of a switch on their way down to the Batmobile.

This colourful sidekick needs an equally colourful outift. Clad in a smart red tunic and very short green shorts, Robin is ready to save the day in style. That's what makes him Batman's best chum and a vital part of the Dynamic Duo!

BATMOBILE
WELL-EQUIPPED WHEELS

VITAL STATS

OWNER: Batman
USED FOR: Foiling diabolical schemes
GEAR: Shooters, grapples

SET NAMES: *Batman* Classic TV Series – Batcave
SET NUMBERS: 76052
YEARS: 2016

Batphone hidden between seats

Dual exhaust pipes

Bazookas for blasting through walls

GRAPPLES AND PAIRS
The trunk of the Batmobile opens to reveal enough room for two grappling hooks and ropes for scaling the sides of buildings, three Batarangs and a pair of handcuffs.

Pow! Blasting out from the Batcave beneath stately Wayne Manor, this gadget-packed Batmobile is the coolest car of the 1960s. Gotham City was pretty different back then, but the Dynamic Duo never go out of fashion!

BATCOPTER
EARLY WHIRLYBIRD

Wings cast a shadow to scare crooks.

Domed cockpit for an all-round view.

MADE FOR TWO
The Boy Wonder takes another seat in the sidecar of this two-person Batcycle. It has space for a handy spare tyre and is also part of the Batman Classic TV Series Batcave set.

Missile in flight

Robin takes the controls of this classic 'copter, which dates from the same time and communicates on the same channel as the Batmobile on p.113. It has wings to aid its flight and shark-repelling missiles for missions at sea!

THE PENGUIN
ANTARCTIC ADVERSARY

VITAL STATS
....
LIKES: Fish and all birds except robins
DISLIKES: Mammals, especially bats
FRIENDS: Catwoman, the Joker, the Riddler
FOES: Batman and Robin
SKILLS: Squawking, scheming
GEAR: Umbrella

SET NAMES: *Batman* Classic TV Series – Batcave
SET NUMBERS: 76052
YEARS: 2016

The Penguin thinks that a top hat makes him look taller.

The Penguin's belly is too big for his tight jacket!

White silk gloves

HIGH AND DRY
When the Penguin sticks his beak into the Batcave, he floats in on his trademark umbrella, which can also shoot knockout gas, cut glass, self-destruct – and even keep the rain off!

Foes don't come fishier than this feather-ruffling ruffian! Waddling his way through the murky waters of Gotham City's underworld, this version of the Penguin is sporting a new lilac-coloured top hat and bow tie!

PIRATE BATMAN
BOOK BUCCANEER

VITAL STATS

LIKES: Buried treasure
DISLIKES: Walking the plank
FRIENDS: The sea
FOES: Brainiac
SKILLS: Swashbuckling
GEAR: Flail, cutlass

SET NAMES: DK's LEGO *DC Comics Character Encyclopedia*
YEARS: 2016

No other Batman minifigure wears this chinless cowl in blue.

Spiked flail for self-defence

Utility Belt worn across chest

BACK THROUGH TIME
Pirate Batman is the only LEGO version so far to feature a bat-symbol on the back of his torso (though it is partly hidden by his piratical Utility Belt).

Curved sword called a cutlass

Shiver me timbers – Batman's a buccaneer! Thrown back in time by Brainiac's Time Ray, this Dark Knight dresses as a pirate to fit in with the seafarers he finds himself amongst. He must rescue Green Lantern before returning to the present day!

189

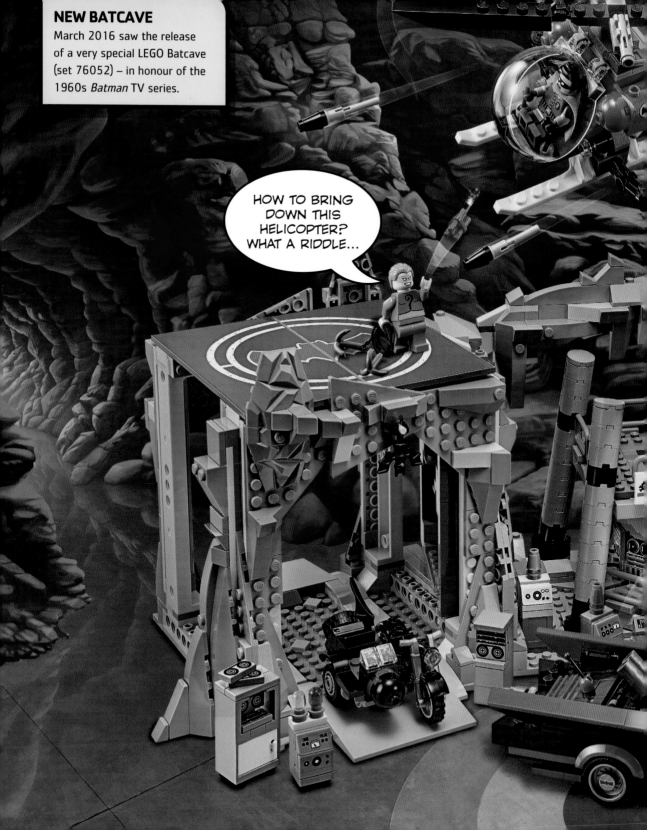

NEW BATCAVE
March 2016 saw the release of a very special LEGO Batcave (set 76052) – in honour of the 1960s *Batman* TV series.

MIGHTY MICROS: CATWOMAN
KITTEN-SIZED CRIMINAL

VITAL STATS

LIKES: Diamonds
DISLIKES: Dogs
FRIENDS: None
FOES: Mighty Micros: Batman
SKILLS: Cat burglary
GEAR: Milk carton

SET NAME: Mighty Micros: Batman vs Catwoman
SET NUMBER: 76061
YEAR: 2016

Cute cat mask disguises a criminal mastermind

Purr-ple lipstick

Belt with cat's-head clasp

Kitten heels

KITTY CAR

Catwoman is the cat who got the cream in her Mighty Micros car. It has cat's eyes and ears between the headlights, and between the taillights – a tail!

This cat always lands on her feet, even though her legs don't bend! Clad in a panther-black catsuit, the feline felon can slip into even the smallest nook or cranny, pilfering everything from priceless jewels to a plate of milk!

MIGHTY MICROS: BATMAN
DIMINUTIVE DARK KNIGHT

VITAL STATS

LIKES: Microscopes
DISLIKES: Micromanagement
FRIENDS: Mighty Micros:
Robin
FOES: Mighty Micros:
Catwoman
SKILLS: Making short work
of villains
GEAR: Batarang

SET NAMES: Mighty Micros:
Batman vs Catwoman
SET NUMBERS: 76061
YEARS: 2016

Determined jaw
under chinless cowl

Utility Belt
holds up
mini tights

Cape flows down
to the ground

Scaled-up bat-symbol
fits with wackier
Mighty Micros universe.

CARTON CAPERS

Batman can snatch stolen milk
from Catwoman's claws in his
Mighty Micros Batmobile. With
a super-speedy afterburner, it's
just the thing for a dairy derby!

The first ever Batman with mini
legs isn't short on crimefighting
skills! He still represents the long
arm of the law, and his cape seems
extra large by comparison. He is
the only Batman minifigure with
different coloured legs and torso.

MIGHTY MICROS: ROBIN
SMALL WONDER

VITAL STATS
....

LIKES: Scaling new heights
DISLIKES: Being grounded
FRIENDS: Mighty Micros: Batman
FOES: Mighty Micros: Bane
SKILLS: Climbing, acrobatics
GEAR: Grapple gun

SET NAMES: Mighty Micros: Bane vs Robin
SET NUMBERS: 76062
YEARS: 2016

Same neat hair as red-suited Robin (p.45)

Mask doesn't hide Robin's happy eyes!

Shorter cape than most Robin minifigures

RELIANT ROBIN

Robin can rely on his Mighty Micros car to get him around on the ground, but he also carries a grapple gun, in case there are any walls to climb!

Non-posable legs

There's nothing at all micro about the smile on this Robin's face! The larger-than-life character couldn't be happier to have his own car for the first time, and he's going to use it to stop Mighty Micros: Bane from causing big trouble in Gotham City!

MIGHTY MICROS: BANE
HE'S GOT A SHORT FUSE

VITAL STATS

LIKES: Drilling tunnels, tunneling drills
DISLIKES: Taking his mask off
FRIENDS: His teddy bear
FOES: Mighty Micros: Robin
SKILLS: Plotting and planning
GEAR: Dynamite

SET NAME: Mighty Micros: Robin vs Bane
SET NUMBER: 76062
YEAR: 2016

Mask hides the tubes that pump Bane full of Venom

No other Bane minifigure wears a top like this

Same black mini legs as Mighty Micros: Batman

JUST A LITTLE BIT

Bane's Mighty Micros drill tank has a shiny rotating drill bit at the front and flaming chimneys at the back. Bane himself lobs dynamite from the driving seat!

The red "B" on his chest stands for Bane, but it could also be for bad, brawny, and brutal! He might not be at his biggest here, but Bane is still one of Batman's most imposing opponents, towering over others in terms of brains and beef!

MIGHTY MICROS: THE FLASH
SHORT-DISTANCE RUNNER

MIGHTY MICROS

VITAL STATS

LIKES: Fast cars
DISLIKES: Dawdlers
FRIENDS: Mighty Micros
Batman, Mighty Micros: Robin
FOES: Mighty Micros:
Captain Cold
SKILLS: Quick thinking
GEAR: Energy drink

SET NAME: Mighty Micros:
The Flash vs Captain Cold
SET NUMBER: 76063
YEAR: 2016

Wings on mask
are a symbol of
speed

All parts of
minifigure are
red – other
colours are
printed.

Small, confident
smile peeks out
from mask

Lightning bolts hint
at how Barry Allen
became The Flash

FLASH DRIVE

This Mighty Micros race car
might not be as fast as The
Flash himself, but it gives his
legs a rest while he enjoys his
can of Power Bolt energy drink!

The Flash loves to stretch his
legs. In fact, he runs so fast, you
can't even see his bottom half
move! The micro marathon man is
hot on the heels of chilly criminal
Captain Cold. He reckons a bit of
exercise should warm him up!

MIGHTY MICROS: CAPTAIN COLD
COMPACT FREEZER

VITAL STATS
....

LIKES: Chilling out
DISLIKES: Global warming
FRIENDS: Snowmen
FOES: Mighty Micros: The Flash
SKILLS: Making ice weapons
GEAR: Freeze gun, snow cone

SET NAME: Mighty Micros:
The Flash vs Captain Cold
SET NUMBER: 76063
YEAR: 2016

Despite his name, Captain Cold likes to wrap up warm.

Cold eyes hidden by thick goggles.

MIGHTY MICROS

DID YOU KNOW?
Captain Cold is the leader of a criminal gang called the Rogues. Its members include the Trickster (see p.165).

PLOWING ON
With a snow cone in one hand and his freeze gun on full blast in the other, Captain Cold uses this Mighty Micros snow plow to find his way through the ice.

Mini legs are frozen stiff!

Look out – there's a mini ice age coming! Ice-cool villain Captain Cold makes his own microclimate with his fearsome freeze gun and his frosty manner. He would love to fast-freeze The Flash in a big block of ice!

INTERVIEW: JOHN CUPPAGE
MODEL DESIGNER

What does it mean to be a LEGO® Model Designer?
I design brick-built models, which could be vehicles, such as the Batmobile or the Riddler's Dragster, but also playsets of buildings and structures within the DC Comics universe. Just recently I have also started designing LEGO® elements, too.

Have you always been a LEGO fan?
I was always a LEGO fan – I have great memories of playing with LEGO sets and DUPLO® sets with my siblings while growing up. A personal highlight for me was the first LEGO Pirates launch in 1989. We played with that range for hours. The Black Seas Barracuda Pirate Ship (set 6285) was my personal favorite.

Black Manta's helmet (from set 76027) was created using the "2K" element moulding technique.

How did you come to work at the LEGO Group?
I never thought that I would work for the LEGO Group! However, I was always creative as a kid and went on to do a Bachelor's degree in Industrial Design in Ireland. I was designing street furniture (such as litterbins and benches) when I made the jump to LEGO toy design! I heard about a Product Design job at the LEGO Group being advertised, so I applied. I was invited to fly out to Denmark for an interview and I got it. It's been a very interesting journey!

How do you plan out the sets alongside DC Comics?
The process varies. Sometimes we might be designing for a particular film or TV series, such as the 2016 *Batman v Superman: Dawn of Justice* movie. In that instance we receive scripts and other reference materials so we can think about what might be fun builds for children. Other times we might want a more classic feel for a set and we take our inspiration directly from DC Comics and their world. In addition, DC Comics might want us to explore particular characters and models. It's a constant dialogue. It also depends on what story we want to tell on the LEGO set box. For example, if we want to create a sub-zero theme set, then it's natural to go straight to Mr Freeze! In another set, Batman: Man-Bat Attack (set 76011), Batman's helicopter is not from any particular movie or cartoon but is totally something that Batman might have in his Batcave!

How do you go about designing and building sets?

We initially brainstorm as a team and propose models, stories, and characters that will make great LEGO sets. We are then assigned to work on a set as an individual designer. This was the case with the 2015 Jokerland set (76035): we all brainstormed and built bits and pieces that might go into a themepark based set. A lot of our decisions come down to what a character's role might be within the set – something might suit one character but not another. For example, the motorcycle within Jokerland really suits Harley Quinn as she's such a daredevil. Equally, the Venus Flytrap elements really work for Poison Ivy.

Are there any exciting new elements that you have designed recently?

We recently designed two cockpit elements, one left and one right, exclusively for the Batman v Superman Batmobile (set 76045) and Batwing (set 76046). They were directly inspired from the way the vehicles look and work in the movie.

In the case of Black Manta Deep Sea Strike (set 76027), for example, this set was not based directly on any specific comic or film. But we still designed a very distinctive helmet for Black Manta himself, trying very hard to make a design that would meet fan expectations and would be a really cool piece. To get this result we used a "2K process" where we mould two different materials together to make one element. Also, when it came to designing Batgirl and her cowl, we could possibly have used Batman's existing cowl, but we wanted to show off her flowing hair, and so we designed a new headpiece, especially for her.

John is pictured with the new Batwing model, appearing in 2016 (set 76046).

Do you have a personal favourite LEGO DC Comics Super Heroes set?

My favorite set would probably have to be the first LEGO set I designed – Arctic Batman vs Mr Freeze: Aquaman on Ice (set 76000) – which will always have a special space in my heart. It's a very cool thing to design a LEGO set when you have had this huge love for LEGO models from when you were a kid. Also, this was really one of the very first sets we designed that explored a different type of mission for Batman with a different style of costume. Plus it has a really fun story to go with it!

Are there any DC Comics characters not yet in LEGO form that you would love to see?

As a kid I was a big Batman fan. And the great thing about Batman is that he has loads of really cool villains to go up against.
I would love to see a LEGO Rā's al Ghūl minifigure. He has a cool story and an interesting dynamic with Batman – respecting him but wanting to defeat him at the same time!

INTERVIEW: ADAM CORBALLY
SENIOR GRAPHIC DESIGNER

What is it like being a LEGO® Graphic Designer?
Being a graphic designer encompasses designing the minifigures and all the minifigure decoration – their expressions, their torsos and legs and also any details on the brick-built models, such as the Batman logo, or stickers and other decorations.

Adam shows off the Batman minifigure from the 2016 sets, with his new armour and boots.

How did you come to work at the LEGO Group?
I happened to be displaying some work at an exhibition in London and the LEGO Group were looking for new graduates so I applied. Since I joined I have mostly worked in the Super Heroes team, but also on other projects such as THE LEGO® MOVIE™, where I really enjoyed designing the "Where Are My Pants" minifigure.

How do you decide which minifigures to make?
There's lots of talk within the design team and with DC about any specific characters that we would want to make and what would be cool. We also bring into the discussion what version of the characters we would like to see – for example, Batman has so many suits: do we want to see him in space with a space suit or does he need an underwater suit for the story we want to tell within the set as a whole?

What's new for LEGO DC Comics Super Heroes?
Our first LEGO DC Comics Super Heroes bigfigs – Darkseid and Gorilla Grodd – were a fun challenge to design as while they are scaled up, they still need to look as cool as a minifigure. For example, Darkseid maintains his minifigure-style eyes. We also got to bring a really fun sense of humour into the Gorilla Grodd set (76026). I enjoyed creating the screaming face for the scared Truck Driver!

Do you have a favourite LEGO DC Comics Super Heroes set?
If I had to choose just one then I'd say Green Lantern vs Sinestro (set 76025). It's such a colourful set, with a bright pink and yellow Sinestro, and it features a Green Lantern minifigure in a set for the first time. Also, the new Batman from this set inspired the Batman from the latest video game. It was a challenge to create those space wings for Batman, with two options for open and closed.

Are there any DC Comics characters not yet in LEGO form that you would love to see?
One minifigure that I really wanted to see before I ever came to work for LEGO DC Comics Super Heroes was Batman of Zur-En-Arrh (San Diego Comic-Con 2014). I love it because we never normally get to see Batman in such bright, wacky colours.

What's next for LEGO DC Comics Super Heroes?
The Batmobile for the new *Batman v Superman: Dawn of Justice* movie is looking really cool. We're all really excited to see what DC Comics will bring to the table.

How do you decide which exclusives to make?
When we talk about characters for books and other exclusive releases we think it has to be really cool – and something that perhaps wouldn't appear in a set. Batman has so many variants, so we work with DC Comics to figure out what we would like to see. For this book we chose Pirate Batman, and used the comics as points of reference.

Graphic Designer Daniel McKenna designs minifigures, such as Pirate Batman.

Daniel McKenna helped to design DK's exclusive, Pirate Batman, and talked to us about the process:
We did a number of designs to begin with, including a Caveman Batman and a Pirate Batman. I loved the zany quirky comedy of the pirate costume contrasted with the seriousness of Batman. We went through several versions to ensure that he remained recognisably and iconically Batman but with fun, piratical elements.

SET GALLERY

A treat for all LEGO® fans, here are all the LEGO DC Comics Super Heroes sets produced so far. How many have you collected? Do you have a favourite? With some exciting new sets releasing in 2016 and beyond, it's time to get them all!

2006

7779
THE BATMAN DRAGSTER:
CATWOMAN PURSUIT

7780
THE BATBOAT: HUNT FOR
KILLER CROC

7781
THE BATMOBILE:
TWO-FACE'S ESCAPE

7782
THE BATWING: THE JOKER'S
AERIAL ASSAULT

7783
THE BATCAVE: THE PENGUIN
AND MR. FREEZE'S INVASION

7784
THE BATMOBILE: ULTIMATE
COLLECTOR'S EDITION

7785
ARKHAM ASYLUM

2007

7786
THE BATCOPTER: THE
CHASE FOR SCARECROW

7787
THE BAT-TANK: THE
RIDDLER AND BANE'S HIDEOUT

2008

7884
BATMAN'S BUGGY: THE
ESCAPE OF MR. FREEZE

7885
ROBIN'S SCUBA JET: ATTACK
OF THE PENGUIN

7886
THE BATCYCLE: HARLEY
QUINN'S HAMMER TRUCK

7888
THE TUMBLER: THE JOKER'S
ICE CREAM SURPRISE

COMCON016
GREEN LANTERN
MINIFIGURE

COMCON017
SUPERMAN
MINIFIGURE

COMCON018
BATMAN
MINIFIGURE

4526
BATMAN

4527
THE JOKER

4528
GREEN LANTERN

6857
THE DYNAMIC DUO
FUNHOUSE ESCAPE

6858
CATWOMAN CATCYCLE
CITY CHASE

6860
THE BATCAVE

6862
SUPERMAN VS
POWER ARMOR LEX

6863
BATWING BATTLE
OVER GOTHAM CITY

6864
BATMOBILE AND THE
TWO-FACE CHASE

30160
BAT JETSKI

30161
BATMOBILE

30164
LEX LUTHOR

COMCON020
SHAZAM! MINIFIGURE

COMCON022
BIZARRO MINIFIGURE

10937

**BATMAN: ARKHAM
ASYLUM BREAKOUT**

76000

**ARCTIC BATMAN VS
MR. FREEZE: AQUAMAN ON ICE**

76001

**THE BAT VS BANE:
TUMBLER CHASE**

76002

**SUPERMAN METROPOLIS
SHOWDOWN**

76003

**SUPERMAN: BATTLE
OF SMALLVILLE**

76009

**SUPERMAN: BLACK
ZERO ESCAPE**

5001623

JOR-EL

**COMCON030
GREEN ARROW MINIFIGURE**

**COMCON029
BLACK SUIT SUPERMAN
MINIFIGURE**

2014

76010
BATMAN: THE
PENGUIN FACE OFF

76011
BATMAN: MAN-BAT ATTACK

76012
BATMAN: THE RIDDLER CHASE

76013
BATMAN: THE JOKER
STEAM ROLLER

76023
THE TUMBLER

5004081
PLASTIC MAN

COMCON036
BATMAN OF ZUR-EN-ARRH

COMCON037
BATMAN CLASSIC TV SERIES BATMOBILE

2015

76025
GREEN LANTERN
VS SINESTRO

76026
GORILLA GRODD
GOES BANANAS

76027
BLACK MANTA DEEP
SEA STRIKE

76028
DARKSEID INVASION

76034
BATBOAT HARBOR PURSUIT

76035
JOKERLAND

76040
BRAINIAC ATTACK

SDCC2015
ACTION COMICS #1 SUPERMAN

SDCC2015
ARSENAL

76044
CLASH OF THE HEROES

76045
KRYPTONITE INTERCEPTION

76046
HEROES OF JUSTICE:
SKY HIGH BATTLE

76052
BATMAN CLASSIC TV
SERIES: BATCAVE

76053
BATMAN: GOTHAM
CITY CYCLE CHASE

76061
MIGHTY MICROS:
BATMAN VS CATWOMAN

76062
MIGHTY MICROS:
ROBIN VS BANE

76063
MIGHTY MICROS:
THE FLASH VS CAPTAIN COLD

Project Editor Emma Grange
Editor Tina Jindal
Senior Designer Nathan Martin
Designer Karan Chaudhary
Editorial Assistant Rosie Peet
**Senior Pre-Production
Producer** Jennifer Murray
Managing Editors Paula Regan,
Simon Hugo, Chitra Subramanyam
Design Managers Neha Ahuja, Guy Harvey
Art Director Lisa Lanzarini
Publisher Julie Ferris
Publishing Director Simon Beecroft

Additional Photography Markos Chouris,
Christopher Chouris, and Gary Ombler

First published in Great Britain in 2016
by Dorling Kindersley,
One Embassy Gardens, 8 Viaduct Gardens, London, SW11 7BW

Page design Copyright © 2020 Dorling Kindersley Limited
A Penguin Random House Company

7 8 9 10 20 21 22 23 24
056-283075-Apr/16

Imported into the EEA by Dorling Kindersley Verlag GmbH.
Arnulfstr. 124, 80636 Munich, Germany.

A CIP catalogue record for this book is available
from the British Library.

ISBN: 978-0-24119-931-2

Printed and bound in China

For the curious

www.LEGO.com
www.dk.com

ACKNOWLEDGEMENTS
DK would like to thank Randi Sørensen,
Paul Hansford, Martin Leighton Lindhardt, Maria
Bloksgaard Markussen, Adam Corbally, Daniel
Mckenna, Casper Glahder, Adam Siegmund Grabowski,
John Cuppage, Justin Ramsden, Karl Oskar Jonas
Norlen, Marcos Bessa, Sally Aston, Sven Robin Kahl,
and Mauricio Bedolla at the LEGO Group, Ben Harper,
Thomas Zellers, and Melanie Swartz at Warner Bros.,
Cavan Scott and Simon Hugo for their writing,
and Sam Bartlett for design assistance.